PAX   XTI

THE WORDS OF
SAINT FRANCIS
AN ANTHOLOGY
COMPILED AND ARRANGED
BY
JAMES MEYER, O.F.M.

FRANCISCAN HERALD PRESS
PUBLISHERS OF FRANCISCAN LITERATURE
CHICAGO, ILLINOIS 60609

Nihil Obstat: Fr. Conradinus Wallbraun O.F.M.
        Censor Librorum
Imprimi Permittitur: Fr. Eligius Weir O.F.M.
        Minister Provincialis
Imprimatur: Samuel Alphonsus Card. Stritch
        Archiepiscopus Chicagiensis
    Die 10 mensis Martii, 1952

INTRODUCTION

THE WORDS OF ST. FRANCIS is intended for
the spiritual benefit of the reader. At the same
time no pains have been spared to supply an
unobjectionable text as well as an exact and
currently idiomatic version. The best texts
available, preferably those of the Quaracchi
editors, have been taken as the basis for a new
translation in the effort to eliminate prevalent
inaccuracies, some of them deplorable. As for
the style, the quaintness affected by so many
when they undertake to write about St. Francis may offer a more or less aesthetic treat, but
it seems to rob the saint's thought of much of
its virile flavor, not seldom of its sense, and
regularly of its telling force as something to
live by.

In a book such as this we must abstract
from fuller critical apparatus analyzing the
words of St. Francis, restricting ourself to the
most indispensable notes; the notes follow the
text in a special section of the book. Scholars
have access to the originals; they are currently indicated.

The *Opuscula S. Patris Francisci* give as fully and correctly as possible the text of what St. Francis *wrote*. We have used the third edition (1949) of the Quaracchi editors. All the writings of St. Francis recognized as authentic by the Quaracchi editors are found in this book. They bear the O symbol.* To understand Francis at his best of earthly and inspired wisdom, one must read each as a whole.

As to what St. Francis *said*, we had to restrict ourself to the significant and lastingly applicable from the saint's life, character and aims, and those of his order; to what is readily quotable, passing up much that is in the nature of the anecdote or episode; to what has been found directly quoted by biographers— indirect quotations of the saint's words would carry much too far and leave too much room for error; to what is found recorded within the first century of St. Francis's death—even later works of this century, such as the *Mirror of Perfection* and the *Fioretti*, show decided embroidery; to what is reasonably authentic

---

*As we go to press, the last and best critical word on the "writings" of St. Francis comes to hand from the Diedrich Coelde-Verlag of Werl i. W., Germany. It is a scholarly disquisition on the character and origin as well as the text and idioms of some twenty-five writings ascribed to St. Francis, with the very latest in critical conclusion incorporated. The authors are two Franciscan Fathers, Drs. Kajetan Esser and Lothar Hardick O.F.M. The title is *Die Schriften des hl. Franziskus von Assisi*—avowedly the first of a series of volumes on Franciscan source material.

—leaving disputed points of fact and text to the scholars.

In a word, as to the sayings of St. Francis, the book is an anthology. The effort has, however, been made to make it poetically if not literally complete, so that what is found quoted directly, will be found satisfactorily representative of all the life and character of St. Francis.

The quotations are, too, so arranged as to give a picture of the life of St. Francis from his conversion to his consummation and his posthumous glory on earth. It is, of course, in no real sense a life—a life would have to do with actions, not words.

Following is a list of abbreviations and symbols used in the book. We call attention to the starred items throughout the book, or rather, to the Notes accompanying them.

1 C.....from Vita Prima or First Life of St. Francis by Thomas of Celano, AN edition, with current paragraph indicated.
2 C.....from Vita Secunda or Second Life, ditto.
AN.....from Analecta Franciscana Vol. X-1, Q.
AR.....from Archivum Franciscanum Historicum, Q.
B......from the Major Legend of St. Bonaventure, AN, with chapter indicated.
BSF....from the Breviary of St. Francis as in TM.

LF . . . . . from the Fioretti or Little Flowers of St. Francis, Passerini text, Firenze, 1907, with current chapter indicated, or the various Considerations on the Stigmata, or other portions.

LTC. . . . from Legend of the Three Companions with current chapter indicated. Faloci-Pulignani text, Foligno, 1898.

MP. . . . . from Speculum Perfectionis or Mirror of Perfection, with chapter indicated; Sabatier (Latin) text, 1923-28, British Society of Fran. Studies.

O . . . . . . from Opuscula, the classic collection of the written works of St. Francis, 3rd edition, 1949, Q, page indicated.

PSV . . . . Passion of S. Verecundus as in TM.

Q . . . . . . published by the Editorial College of Quaracchi.

SdB . . . . from Stephen of Bourbon as in TM.

TJC . . . . Testimony of Joseph Coppoli as in TM.

TM. . . . . Minor Testimonies of the XIIIth Century, Lemmens, Q.

TRM . . . Treatise on the Miracles of St. Francis by Thomas of Celano, AN, with paragraph indicated.

* . . . . an asterisk refers the reader to the Notes in the rear of the book under the current number.

(. . .) . . . numbers found in the text, merely in bold type or also enclosed in parentheses, indicate cross references to the respective entries in the text.

TABLE OF CONTENTS

*The numbers indicated in parentheses are the marginal num-
bers of the several entries; for easy reference the marginal
numbers found on any two opposite pages throughout the
book are indicated at the top of the right-hand page at the
inner margin.

Part 1

Saint Francis Entertains Ideals

PART I

St. Francis entertains ideals

IT WAS GIVEN TO St. Francis by God ever to aspire to what was great and best as he saw it at the time. That held from his youthful aspiration to knighthood, on through his life of renunciation, to his complete final self-immorlation.

1. Military, knightly glory first led him, sustained doubtless by his mother's oft-expressed conviction that her Francis should one day be a great prince. And he was the King of Revels to Assisi's youth.

But early another note began creeping in: in prison at Perugia, half in fun half in earnest, it was:

"Why do you think I am so happy-hearted? I have other matter to think about. Some day I am going to be venerated throughout the world as a saint."—2C 4.

2. Not that earthly dreams now left him. On his crusade to Apulia the vision asked him, "Who can do more for you, a servant or the master?" Characteristic was Francis' response:

"What is it you want me to do, Lord?"

Said the vision: "Go back to your home

3

country, for your vision will be fulfilled there
spiritually by me."

After his return a happy Francis would tell
people he would be a great prince some day.—
2C 6, LTC 2.

3. Francis did not remain under the illusion.
Abstracted in the midst of his revels one day, he
makes the sudden baffling statement to his
teasing questioners:

"I *am* going to marry a bride, one nobler
and fairer than any you have ever seen, one
that will be outstanding for beauty and will
impress everybody else for wit."—1C 7.

4. A definitely spiritual ideal, it begins taking
proper shape when at St. Damian's the Crucified
tells him to repair the crumbling house of God.
He says:

"Gladly will I do it, Lord."—LTC 5.

And he proceeds to beg stones and to repair
the walls, giving the priest money for a lamp to be
kept burning before the Crucifix, as generous to
his Lord as he had been to his boon companions
and still the fair-dealing draper's clerk:

"Whoever gives me one stone, shall have
one reward, but whoever gives me two stones,
shall have two rewards, yes and whoever gives
me three stones, he shall have three rewards."
—LTC 7.

5. There was need for generosity, for suffering
was to bring out the best in Francis. As it should
be, his father was the man to introduce him to
the lady of his choice, to the Lady Poverty,

though Francis himself did not realize that till later. Heavy fell the strokes, but no heart ever more willing than that of Francis. To his wrathful father:

"Here I am. I do not mind your locking me up or beating me. I am glad to suffer any evil at all in the name of Christ."—1C 13.

6. Soon it is:

"From now on I shall be free to say, 'Our Father who are in Heaven,' and no longer, 'Father Peter Bernardone.' To him right here I now not only return his money but give up all my clothes. Thus, naked will I go my way to the Lord."—2C 12.

7. To the bandits, as he goes forth:

"I am a herald of the Great King."

He pays with a snow bath for that dedicatory declaration.—1C 16.

8. When his brother, seeing Francis shiver at his prayers in the cold, prompts someone to ask him for a penny's worth of his sweat:

"Indeed I am going to sell that, and very dearly, to my Lord."—2C 12.

9. He begins to recognize the Lady Poverty, now constantly at his side. Even what he can have, he gives up:

"You will not always find this priest about, to keep supplying you with such alms. That is no life for a person professing poverty. It is not good for you to get accustomed to such treatment; you will gradually return to what you have spurned and go yearning again for delicacies. Get right up now and beg from door to door for your mixed victuals."— 2C 14.

10. Gradually he came to recognize his lady's royal quality:

"The Son of God was nobler than we, and he made himself poor in this world for our sake. For love of him we have chosen the path of poverty; we ought not to be embarrassed at going out for alms. It is in no way fitting for the heirs of the Kingdom to blush over the token of their heavenly inheritance. I tell you there will be many noble, learned men joining our company who will take it as an honor to beg for alms. You, therefore, who are the first-fruits of them, be glad, feel happy, and do not refuse to do the things you are handing down to those holy men to do."—2C 74.

11. Again:

"Understand that poverty is a choice way of salvation; the fruit it bears is manifold, and rare are they who know it well."

He called it the "royal virtue," since it shone forth so exceptionally in Christ the King, and Mary the Queen.—2C 200.

12. "It is poverty which makes people

heirs and kings of the Kingdom of Heaven, not your false riches."—2C 72.

13. To Cardinal Ugolino, who was hurt that Francis begged alms while his guest—playfully:

"Rather, I have shown you honor by giving honor to a greater Lord in your house. For that Lord takes great pleasure in poverty, especially in the form of voluntary begging, while I possess a regal dignity and a distinguished nobility when I imitate the Lord, who, rich as he was, became poor for our sake, . . . I get more satisfaction out of a poor table set with little alms than out of grand tables with almost countless dishes."—2C 73.

14. If Lady Poverty left him and his followers nothing to offer the world in return but what is implied in the greeting, "The Lord give you peace":

"Do not be ashamed of it, for the day will come when the nobles and princes of this world will show reverence to you and the rest of the brothers on account of this greeting. It is nothing to marvel at if the Lord should wish to have some new little company as his own, to be apart and different in word and life from all who have gone before it, if it in turn be content to hold Him as its most high, dear and glorious own."—MP 26.

15. The same note of Lady Poverty leading hosts with him recurs to him whose youthful dream was of leadership:

"Take courage, dearest brothers, and rejoice in the Lord. And do not be sad because
you seem to be few, and do not let my plain-
ness or yours discourage you; because, as the
Lord has actually shown me, God is going to
make us grow into a very great multitude and
spread us out in numbers to the ends of the
earth. For your benefit too I am forced to tell
what I have seen, and yet I would much
rather keep silent about it, if charity did not
force me to relate it to you.

"I have seen a great multitude of people
coming to us and wishing to associate with us
in our habit of holy conduct and our rule for a
blessed religious life. Why, there is still in my
ears the sound of them going and coming at
the order of holy obedience. I have seen the
roads so to say of every nation coming together hereabouts, filled with the multitude of
them. Natives of France are coming, Spaniards hurrying along, Germans and English-
men a-running, and a very great multitude of
the various other tongues making haste."—
1C 27.

16. In time his appreciation of Lady Poverty
grew so romantic that a devoted son of his did
well to dramatize his praises of her as described
by other sons*, in

THE RHAPSODY OF LADY POVERTY

"O Lord Jesus, show me the paths of your
dearly beloved Poverty. For I know that the

Old Testament is the figure of the New, and
to them of old you promised that 'every place
in which your foot will tread, shall be yours'
(Deut. 11, 24). To tread on anything is to
despise it. Poverty treads on everything, so it
is the queen of everything.

"But, O dear Lord Jesus Christ, take pity
on me and the Lady Poverty, for I am full of
anxiety in my love for her and cannot calm
myself away from her. You know it, my Lord,
for you have enamored me of her. But there
she is, sitting in sadness, rejected by everybody. She, 'the sovereign Lady of the Nations,
has become like a widow woman' (Lam. 1, 1),
base and abject though she is Queen of the
Virtues, and seated on a dunghill she com-
plains that all her friends have spurned her
and become her enemies, showing for so long
a time now that they are unfaithful and not
true spouses.

"See, Lord Jesus, Poverty is to that extent
the Queen of the Virtues that you left the
haunts of the angels and came down on earth
so you could betroth her to you in everlasting love and beget all the children of perfection in Poverty, and of it, and through it. And
Poverty clung to you so faithfully that she
began her service to you in the very womb of
your mother, where you had of all living
bodies the tiniest. Then too as you came forth
from the womb, she welcomed you to the

holy manger and the stable, and as you went about in the world, she kept you so despoiled of everything that she had you do without a place to rest your head.

"But also she went with you faithfully as your most loyal companion when you undertook the battle for our redemption. In the very clash of your suffering she was there as your inseparable armor-bearer, and though the disciples deserted you and denied knowing you, she did not abandon you but stayed faithfully at your side with all the company of her noble peers. Yes when, because the cross was so high, your very Mother—and such a Mother!—could not reach you (though she cherished you faithfully even then and remained in union with your sufferings with anguished affection)—then, I say, Lady Poverty was there like a most welcome handmaiden with all her privations to enfold you more tightly than ever and to share the more feelingly in your torment.

"That is why she took no time to smoothen the cross or to provide it with even crude comfort. The very nails, it is believed, she did not supply in sufficient number for the wounds, nor sharpen them and polish them, but had only three coarse, rough, dull nails ready to add to your cruel pain. And when you were tortured with that intense thirst, she was there with the concern of a faithful spouse to see that you could have not even a bit of water, but she had the heartless hangmen fix up a drink so bitter that you could rather taste of it than drink it. And so it was that you gave forth your spirit in the tight embrace of this your spouse.

"Your faithful spouse, however, was not absent either at your funeral rites, and permitted you to have nothing but what was borrowed for your tomb, your ointments and your burial cloths. Neither was your holy spouse missing at your resurrection, since, as you rose gloriously in her embrace, you left all that was loaned and foreign behind you in the tomb. Finally, you took her to Heaven with you, leaving to the people of the world everything that is of the world. And then you consigned to Lady Poverty the seal of the kingdom of Heaven, to mark with that seal the elect who desire to fare along the path of perfection.

"Oh, who would not love this your Lady Poverty above all others! I entreat you for the favor of being sealed with this privilege, I crave to be enriched with this treasure. I beg you, O Jesus most poor, that it may be the distinction of me and mine forevermore, for your name's sake to possess nothing under heaven as our own and to be sustained as long as our poor flesh lives only with the closely restricted use of things given us by others."

Little wonder that St. Francis found he could really say he had five Lesser Brothers when the news broke of the five brothers martyred in Morocco: they really had given everything they had back to God!

17. Little wonder Francis saw Lady Poverty as more than renunciation of property: everything must go with it, until you are like your Savior:

"So great the good I have in sight,

That any pain is my delight."—LF 1st Stigm.

18. Little wonder that he came to have the generous ideal which was rehearsed on the way with Brother Leo, telling of

PERFECT JOY

"Brother Leo, were it to please God that the Lesser Brothers gave in every country a grand example of holiness and edification in virtue, nevertheless write it down and take careful note of it: there is not perfect joy in that."

And a little farther on:

"O Brother Leo, though a Lesser Brother give sight to the blind, straighten the limbs of the crippled, drive out demons, give hearing to the deaf, make the lame walk, give speech to the mute, and still more, raise up the four-day dead, write down that there is not perfect joy in that."

Still farther on:

"O Brother Leo, if a Lesser Brother knew all the languages and all the sciences and all the Scriptures, so that he could prophesy and reveal not only things future but also the secrets of consciences and minds, write, that perfect joy lies not in that."

Then again, with a loud voice:

"O Brother Leo, little lamb of God, though your Lesser Brother spoke the language of the angels and knew the course of the stars and the virtues of the herbs; and there were disclosed to him all the treasures of the earth, and he knew the characteristics of the birds and the fish and the animals, and of men, and of trees and stones and roots and waters: write that perfect joy is not in that."

And later:

"O Brother Leo, though your Lesser Brother could preach so well as to convert all the infidels to the Faith of Christ: write that perfect joy is not in that."

At length, at Brother Leo's impatient demand:

"If we get to St. Mary's of the Angels so drenched with rain and frozen with cold and spattered with mud and afflicted with hunger, and knock at the door of the place*and the porter comes in anger and says, Who are you? and we say, We are two of your brothers; and if he says, You are not telling the truth, you are rather two loafers who are going about fooling the world and robbing the alms of the poor—get out!; and he does not open the door for us, and makes us stay outdoors in the snow and rain amid the cold and our hunger, till nightfall; then if we endure all those insults and cruelties and rebuffs patiently and without being ruffled or murmuring at him; and we humbly and charitably think that this porter really knows us but that God is having him talk up to us that way: oh, Brother Leo, write that there is perfect joy in that.

"And if we go on knocking, and he comes out all wrought up and drives us away with abusive language, and cuffs us as if we were impudent clods, saying, Get out of here, you low-down thievish fellows, go on to the hostel, for you will get neither bite nor bed here; if we take that patiently, with good cheer and charity: Oh, Brother Leo, write that therein there is perfect joy.

"And if we, still forced by hunger, cold and the darkness go on rapping and asking for the love of God amid many tears that he should open and let us in and he, more outraged than before, says: Now, these fellows are impudent oafs, and I am going to pay them out as they deserve; and he comes out with a

knotted cudgel, grabs us by the cowl, flings us
on the ground, rolls us about in the snow,
and beats us joint by joint with that cudgel;
if we took all this punishment patiently and
with good cheer, thinking of it as the sufferings of Christ the blest which we ought to
bear for his love: oh, Brother Leo, write down
that therein there is perfect joy.

"And now listen to the conclusion, Brother
Leo. Above all the graces and gifts of the
Holy Ghost which Christ grants his friends,
there is that of overcoming themselves and
gladly for the love of Christ bearing pain,
insults, disgrace, and discomfort, because we
cannot glory in any of the other gifts of God
—they are not ours, but God's. Therefore the
Apostle says: 'What have you that you have
not received from God? And if you have
received it from God, why do you glory as if
you had not received it?'

"But in the cross of tribulation and affliction we may glory because that is our due,
and so the Apostle says: 'I do not wish to
glory in anything but in the cross of our Lord
Jesus Christ.' To whom ever be honor and
glory world without end. Amen."—LF 8.

Only, would such a Francis refuse the cross of a
crisis such as came in the last years of his life?
When he was asked to surrender something of his

ideal in order to save the entire fabric, at the urging of his beloved Mother Church?

19. So complete was St. Francis's immolation for his Lord's love that he finally asked for what amounts to crucifixion with his Lord:

"O Lord Jesus Christ, I entreat you to give me two graces before I die: first, that in my lifetime I may feel in body and soul as far as possible the pain you endured, dear Lord, in the hour of your most bitter suffering; and second, that I may feel in my heart as far as possible that excess of love by which you, O Son of God, were inflamed to undertake so cruel a suffering for us sinners."—LF 3rd Stigm.

The Stigmata were the answer—the culmination on earth of the ideal St. Francis!*

Part II

Saint Francis
Addresses himself
to God

PART II

St. Francis addresses himself to God

Happy for St. Francis that his mind turned so readily to God! In the holy ambitions he had, only his consciousness of utter dependence on God could keep him from extravagance and aberration. The thought of God, however, was with him as a vital force even before his conversion.

20. Witness the day he absent-mindedly rebuffed a beggar asking alms for the love of God:

"Had this poor man asked you for something in the name of some distinguished count or baron, you certainly would have given him his request. How much more ought you do it for the King of Kings and the Lord of all things?"—LTC 1.

21. He would say to himself:

"If you are so bountiful and polite toward people from whom you receive only a passing empty favor, it is no more than decent for you to be polite and bountiful toward God, who is so bounteous in giving to his poor."
—LTC 1.

22. When the test came, his thoughts went spontaneously to God, as we have already seen in Part I. Now God became his preoccupation, first in quest of light and strength, inarticulate, then however more and more selfless on to total immolation. Through the night at Bernard of Quintavalle's house, it was:

"My God, my God!"—LF 2.

23. More often there were whole nights of:

"My God and my all!"*

—which extended itself to:

"My God and my all! Who are you, O God most dear, and who am I, your worthless, useless little worm of a servant!"—LF 3rd Stigm.

To which Fr. Bartholomew of Pisa (I Bk. of Conf. 8) adds:

"Most holy Lord, I should like to love you. Dearest God, I should like to love you. O Lord God, I have given up to you all my heart and my body, and I yearn passionately to do still more for love of you if only I knew how."

24. If he knew how! He used to say the words of Psalm 142, 10:

"You are my God, teach me to do your will."—1C 6.

25. This prayer was said by him in the beginning of his conversion:

"O great God of glory, my Lord Jesus Christ, I entreat you, put light into the darkness of my mind. Give me the right faith, firm hope, and perfect charity. Help me learn to know you, O Lord, so well that in all things I may do everything in true keeping with your holy will."—*Opera Omnia S.P.N. Francisci,* Wadding—de la Haye, p. 18.

26. His selflessness becomes more complete as his thought of our Lord turns to pity for him ("Love is not loved!"):

"I weep over the sufferings of my Lord Jesus Christ, and I ought not to be ashamed to go all over the world weeping out loud, for his sake."—LTC 5.

27. His thought as brothers join him in the order is to ask God for due fervor for himself and for them.

"Lord, be merciful to me a sinner."—1C 26.

28. The thought of his brothers was with him in his prayers:

"Almighty, eternal, just, and merciful God, have us poor wretches for your sake do what we know you want, and have us always want whatever is pleasing to you; so that cleansed interiorly, and interiorly enlightened and aglow with the fire of the Holy Ghost, we may be able to follow the footsteps of your Son, our Lord Jesus Christ. Aided by your sole-saving grace may we be able to get to you, who in perfect Trinity and simple Unity live and reign and triumph as God almighty world without end. Amen."—O 107.

29. Here belongs also the extended prayer forming the greater part of Chapter 23 in the First Rule as in **283-9**.

30. Francis was happy at the virtue of his brothers, but referred it to God:

"I give you thanks, O Lord, who sanctify and govern the poor, for making me happy with such a report about my brothers. I beseech you, bless those brothers with your most bounteous blessing and sanctify with a special gift all whose good example gives their profession a good odor."—2C 178.

31. Keenly aware before God was he of the brothers' responsibility:

"O Lord Jesus Christ, you chose your apostles twelve in number. And though one of the number fell, the rest clung to you and preached the holy Gospel, filled with one spirit. You, O Lord, in this last hour, mindful of your olden mercy, have planted this order of brothers as a prop of your Faith and as a means to fulfil the mystery of the Gospel through them.

"Now, who is to make up for them before you if they not only fail to demonstrate before everybody the example of light, for which purpose they have been sent, but rather display the works of darkness?"

Then, as if even now one with God on Doomsday, as we all shall be on that day:

"By you, most holy Lord, and by all the court of Heaven, and by poor little me, let them be cursed who by their bad example embarrass and destroy what you have once built up and do not cease to build up through holy brethren of this order!"—2C 156.

32. This was his prayer when illness and trouble bore in on him:

"Lord, take pity on my infirmities, so that I may be able to bear them patiently."—MP 100.

33. Yet not in faint-heartedness, but in the spirit of the following beautiful prayer, the Absorbeat:

"Please, O Lord, let the fiery, honeyed force of your love lap up my spirit from everything there is under Heaven: so that I may die for love of love for you, who deigned to die for love of love for me."—O 125.

34. For Brother Leo's benefit Francis one day wrote down a prayer which shows what depths of mysticism Francis had sounded:*

PAGE OF PRAISES FOR BR. LEO

"You alone are holy, O Lord God, you are he who performs things wondrous.

You are strong. You are full of majesty. You are the most high.

You are the King Almighty—you, holy Father, King of Heaven and Earth.

You are the Lord God, threefold and one, all that is good.

You are what is good, all that is good, the Sovereign Good, the Lord God true and living.

You are charity and love. You are widsom.

You are humility. You are patience. You are assurance. You are restfulness.

You are joy and gladness. You are justice and temperance.

You are all the wealth desirable. You are beauty. You are gentleness.

You protect. You guard and defend.

You are fortitude. You are refreshment.

You are our hope. You are our faith. You are our great relish.

You are our eternal life, great and wondrous Lord, God almighty, Savior merciful."

35. Brother Leo himself was blessed by Francis with the blessing from Numbers 6, 24:

"May the Lord bless you and keep you.

May he show his face to you and have mercy on you.

May he turn his countenance toward you and give you peace.

The Lord bless—Brother † Leo—you." — O 124.

36. Similar depths and heights are disclosed in St. Francis's paraphrase of the Our Father with accompanying Praises and Oration, called the Praises of God in the Our Father or simply the Lauds or the Praises. As found in the Assisi manuscript they begin with a note telling that St. Francis said them at every Hour of the day and night and before he said the Little Office of the Bl. Virgin. As is seen, they consist of a paraphrase of the Our Father followed by certain passages of Holy Scripture in praise of God. We indicate Scriptural references currently.

THE PRAISES OF GOD IN THE OUR FATHER

"Our Father most holy: our Creator, our Redeemer and Savior, our Comforter.

"Who are in Heaven: in the angels and the saints, giving them light to know you, since you, O Lord, are Light; setting them afire to love you, since you, O Lord, are Love; abiding in them and filling them for their bliss, since you, O Lord, are the sovereign good, the eternal good, from which everything good has its being and without which there is nothing good.

"Hallowed be your name: may we grow in our knowledge of you, that we may appreciate the width of your favors and the length of your promises to us as well as the utter height of your majesty and the depth of your judgments (cf. Eph. 3, 18).

"*Your kingdom come:* so that you may rule in us through grace and have us get to your kingdom, where the sight of you is clear, love of you is perfect, association with you is full of bliss, and enjoyment of you is eternal.

"*Your will be done on earth as it is in Heaven:* so that we may love you with all ou. heart by always keeping you in mind; with all our soul by always longing for you; with all our mind by directing all our intentions to you and seeking your glory in everything; and with all our strength by exerting all the forces and faculties of soul and body in your loving service and in nothing else. So may we love our neighbors as ourselves, by getting them all so far as we can to love you, by being as glad at the good fortune of others as at our own, while feeling for their misfortune, and giving no offense to anybody (cf. 2 Cor. 6, 3).

"*Give us this day*—so that we will remember, understand and respect the love he bore for us and all he said and did and endured for us—*our daily bread*—your beloved Son, our Lord Jesus Christ.

"*And forgive us our debts:* in your unutterable mercy, in virtue of the suffering of your beloved Son, our Lord Jesus Christ, and at the merits and intercession of the blessed Virgin Mary and all your elect.

"*As we forgive our debtors:* and what we do not fully forgive, do you, O Lord, make us forgive fully, so that for your sake we may truly love our enemies and devotedly intercede with you for them, giving nobody evil in return for evil and trying to be helpful toward everybody in your name.

"*And lead us not into temptation:* neither hidden nor apparent, neither sudden nor persistent.

"*But deliver us from evil:* past, present, and future. Amen.

"Glory be to the Father, etc.

36a. "Holy, holy, holy, the Lord God almighty, who is, and who was, and who is to come (Apoc. 4, 8). Let us praise and exalt him above all things forever (cf. Dan. 3, 57).

"You are worthy, O Lord our God, to receive praise, and glory, and honor, and blessing (Apoc. 4, 11). Let us praise and exalt him above all things forever.

"Worthy is the Lamb who was slain, to receive power and godhead and wisdom and strength and honor and glory and blessing (Apoc. 5, 12). Let us praise and exalt him above all things forever.

"Let us bless the Father and the Son with the Holy Ghost. Let us praise and exalt him above all things forever.

"Bless the Lord, all you works of the Lord (Dan. 3, 57). Let us praise and exalt him above all things forever.

"Speak your praise to God, all his servants and all you who fear the Lord, little and great (Apoc. 19, 5). Let us praise and exalt him above all things forever.

"May the heavens and the earth praise him in his glory—and every creature in Heaven and on earth and under the earth together with the sea and everything in it. (Apoc. 5, 13). Let us praise and exalt him above all things forever.

"Glory be to the Father and to the Son and to the Holy Ghost. Let us praise and exalt him above all things forever.

"As it was in the beginning, is now, and ever shall be world without end. Amen. Let us praise and exalt him above all things forever.

36b. "Prayer: Almighty, most holy, most high and sovereign God, the sovereign good, everything that is good, wholly good, who alone are good: to you let us render all praise, all glory, all thanks, all honor, all blessing, and to you let us refer always whatever is good. Amen."

37. But all the warmth of the prayerful heart of St. Francis is poured out in his Office of the Passion of Our Lord.

The "psalms" of this Passion Office are made up for the greater part of single verses or parts of verses taken almost exclusively from the Book of the Psalms. Occasionally St. Francis adds his own heart's effusion. We indicate the sources currently with the number of psalm and verse, or with the initials plus chapter and verse of other Scripture texts, while St. Francis's own words appear in italics. Most of the verses are spoken in the person of Christ addressing his Father. In the division of the verses we follow the Quaracchi editors (—O p. 126-148).

The Office of the Passion is arranged in five settings as indicated more exactly in the text: 1.) For the last two days of Holy Week and the weekdays of the year; 2.) for the Easter season; 3.) for the Sundays and principal feasts of the year; 4.) for Advent; 5.) for Christmas time to the close of the octave of Epiphany. Except for Christmas, at First Vespers, the Office for each day begins with the Compline and goes on through (second) Vespers. The year's cycle begins with the Compline on Holy Thursday itself, "because on that night our Lord Jesus Christ was betrayed and taken prisoner."

Notes in the Assisi manuscript of the Office of the Passion tell how St. Francis used to say the Office:

a. He would begin with the recitation of the Office by saying the Lauds or Praises found in this volume just above (**36**).

b. Then he would say the initial words of the antiphon: "Holy Virgin Mary."

c. Next he said the respective "Psalms of St. Mary" (the Little Office of the Blessed Virgin? the M-A-R-I-A psalms?); after which came other Scripture psalms of his choice.

d. Then came the psalm he had specially compiled or selected for the Office of the Passion, as hereafter to follow.

e. He ended each psalm with the "Glory be to the Father," etc. Then he said the entire antiphon:

37a. "Holy Virgin Mary, there was never anyone like you born in the world among women—daughter and handmaid of the most high King, our Father in Heaven; mother of our most holy Lord Jesus Christ; spouse of the Holy Ghost! With the archangel St. Michael and all the Virtues of Heaven and all the saints pray for us at the throne of your beloved most holy Son, our Lord and Master."

f. This was followed with a final "Glory be to the Father," etc.

g. On finishing the Office St. Francis would say:

37b. "Let us bless the Lord, the true and living God. To him let us accord praise, glory, honor, blessing, and all good things forever. Amen, amen. So be it, so be it."

Of course it is a matter of each person's devotion just how much and what of the Office he will choose to say. We suggest as the integral parts what is comprised under b, d, e, f, and g just above. We leave it to the devout reader to supply the parts b, e, f and g; they are to be repeated with each hour.

The rubrics found in the original are not in the words of St. Francis: we have tried to simplify **them.**

OFFICE OF THE PASSION OF OUR LORD
First Office

For the Compline on Holy Thursday itself, for Good Friday, for Holy Saturday through the Vespers. Also for all weekdays beginning with the Compline on Trinity Sunday and going through the Vespers on the Saturday before the first Sunday of Advent; and beginning with the Compline on the Octave day of Epiphany through the Vespers on Holy Saturday.

Psalm for Compline:

37c. My life I have made known to you, O God ★ you have my tears set down in your sight (55, 9).

All my enemies were ranged against me to devise evil on me (40, 8) ★ they went into council together (70, 10).

And they lodged evil against me in return for my favors ★ and hatred for the love I gave them (108, 5).

Instead of giving me love, they defamed me ★ but I had recourse to prayer (108, 4).

My holy Father, King of heaven and earth, do not leave me ★ for tribulation is close at hand, and there is no one to help me (21, 12).

My foes shall reel backward whatever the day I invoke you ★ see, I have learned that you are my God (55, 10).

My friends and my neighbors came toward me and halted ★ and those close to me took their stand afar off (37, 12).

Those who know me, you kept at a distance, they hold me a thing to be loathed ★ I was yielded up, and had no way to escape (87, 9).

Holy Father, stand not far off from me with your help ★ my God, give heed to helping me (21, 20).

Be mindful to assist me ★ O Lord, God of my salvation (37, 23).

Psalm for Matins:

37d. Lord, God of my salvation ★ day and night have I cried out before you (87, 2).

May my prayer enter your presence★ bend your ear to my pleading (87, 3).

Be intent on my soul and deliver it ★ because of my enemies, snatch me away (68, 19).

For it is you who brought me forth from the womb, who have been my hope from the breasts of my mother ★ from her womb have I been cast upon you (21, 10).

From the womb of my mother forward, you are my God (21, 11) ★ do not depart from me (21, 12).

You know my reproach and my confusion ★ and the shame confronting me (68, 20).

Your sight takes in all those afflicting me ★ my heart has looked forward to reproach and misery (68, 21).

And I waited for someone to grieve with me, but there was none ★ and for someone to comfort me, and I found none (68, 21).

The wicked, O God, have risen against me and the mighty assembled have been seeking my life ★ and you they have not kept in sight (85, 14).

I am rated with those who go down to the pit ★ become like a man beyond help, my place among the dead (87, 5).

You are my Father most holy ★ *my King and my God.*

Be mindful to assist me ★ O Lord, God of my salvation (37, 23).

Psalm for the Prime:

37e. Have mercy on me, O God, have mercy on me ★ for my soul places its trust in you (56, 1).

And in the shadow of your wings I shall have hope ★ until wickedness passes away (56, 2).

I will cry to *my most holy Father most high* ★ to God, who has been good to me (56, 3).

He has sent help from Heaven to rescue me ★ he has delivered to shame those who trod upon me (56, 4).

He has shown his mighty and faithful hand (56, 4), he has snatched up my soul from my strongest enemies and those who hate me ★ for they grew too strong for me (17, 18).

They laid a snare for my feet ★ and brought my soul low (56, 7).

They dug a pit in my path ★ and fell into

it themselves (56. 7).

My heart is ready, O God, my heart is ready ★ I will sing and intone a psalm (56, 8).

Awake, O my soul, awake, harp and viol ★ I will arise at the dawn (56, 9).

I will give praise to you, O Lord, among the nations ★ I will sing a psalm to you among the Gentiles (56, 10).

For your mercy looms up to the very heavens ★ and your fidelity to the very clouds (56, 11).

Be exalted, O God, above the heavens ★ and your glory spread all over the earth (56, 12).

Psalm for the Tierce:

37f. Have mercy on me, O God, for man has trodden me under foot ★ all the day long he troubles me with his assaults (55, 2).

My foes have trodden me under foot all the day long ★ for many are those at war against me (55, 3).

All my enemies have been devising evil against me ★ they laid their wicked plan against me (40, 8-9).

As they lay in wait for my soul ★ they took counsel together (70, 10).

And as they went forth ★ they spoke to the same purpose (40, 7).

All who saw me, laughed at me ★ they mouthed at me and shook their head (21, 8).

But I am a worm and no man ★ a by-word among people and the outcast of the rabble (21, 7).

Far more than all my enemies have I become a reproach to my neighbors ★ and something for my acquaintance to dread (30, 12).

Holy Father, stand not far off from me with your help ★ have regard for my defense (21, 20).

Be mindful to assist me ★ O Lord, God of my salvation (37, 23).

Psalm for the Sext:

37g. With a loud voice I cried to the Lord ★ with a loud voice I made entreaty before the Lord (141, 2).

I keep pouring out my prayer in his sight ★ and voicing my tribulation before him (141, 3).

While my spirit is failing within me ★ still you know of my farings (141, 4).

On the very road I was walking ★ they hid a snare for me (141, 4).

I peered to my right and stood looking ★ and there was no one who would recognize me (141, 5).

Flight is at an end for me ★ and there is no one to be concerned about my life (141, 5).

For your sake I have borne the disgrace ★ and shame has covered my face (68, 8).

I have become a stranger to my own brothers ⋆ and an alien to the sons of my mother (68, 9).

Holy Father, zeal for your house has eaten me up ⋆ and the revilings of your scoffers have fallen on me (68, 10).

They were gleeful at me and gathered together ⋆ scourges were heaped on me and I knew not the reason (34, 15).

Greater than the hairs of my head is the number ⋆ of those who hate me without cause (68, 5).

Strong have my enemies grown, who wrongfully persecute me ⋆ I paid then for what I took not away (68, 5).

Evil witnesses stood up and made question ⋆ of things I know naught about (34, 11).

They repaid me with evil for good (34, 12) and defamed me ⋆ because I pursued what was good (37, 21).

You are my Father most holy ⋆ *my King and my God.*

Be mindful to assist me ⋆ O Lord, God of my salvation (37, 23).

Psalm for the None:

37h. Oh, all you who pass by the way ⋆ pause and see whether there be sorrow like my sorrow (Lam. 1, 12).

For hounds in number surround me ⋆ a council of malicious men has beset me (21, 17).

But they have turned their eyes and stared

at me (21, 18) ★ they have divided my garments among them and cast lots for my robe (21, 19).

They have dug holes in my hands and my feet (21, 17) ★ they have numbered all my bones (21, 18).

They have opened their mouth against me ★ like a lion ravening and roaring (21, 14).

I am poured out like water ★ and all my bones are disjointed (21, 15).

My heart has become like molten wax ★ in the midst of my body (21, 15).

My strength is dried up like earthenware ★ and my tongue has stuck in my throat (21, 16).

And for food they gave me gall ★ and in my thirst they gave me vinegar to drink (68, 22).

To the dust of death they brought me low (21, 16) ★ and they kept adding to the pain of my wounds (68, 27).

I slept and I rose again ★ and *my Father most holy welcomed me with glory* (3, 6).

You, *holy Father*, have taken my right hand ★ and at your pleasure you led me on and took me up in glory (72, 24).

For what have I in Heaven ★ and besides you what do I desire on earth? (72, 25).

Behold, behold that I am God, says the Lord ★ I shall be exalted among the nations, I shall be exalted on earth (45, 11).

Blest is the Lord, the God of Israel, who has redeemed the souls of his servants *with his own most holy blood* ★ and all who hope in him shall not offend (33, 23).

And we know that he is coming ★ coming to judge with justice (95, 13).

Psalm for Vespers:

37i.   Oh, clap your hands, you nations all ★ acclaim your God with a voice of exultation (46, 2).

For the Lord is high aloft, and worthy of awe ★ the great King over all the earth (46, 3).

For the most holy Father in Heaven, our King, before time sent his beloved Son from on high ★ and he has wrought salvation in the midst of the earth (73, 12).

Let the heavens rejoice, and the earth exult, and the sea be stirred and all that fills it (95, 11) ★ the fields shall be glad and everything in them (95, 12).

Sing to him a new chant ★ sing, all the earth, to the Lord (95, 1).

For great is the Lord and greatly to be praised ★ he is worthy of awe above all gods (95, 4).

Bring to the Lord, you homes of the nations, bring honor and glory to the Lord (95, 7) ★ bring glory to the Lord for his name (95, 8).

Make sacrifice of your person and carry his

holy cross ★ *and follow his most holy precepts even to the end.*

Let all the earth be stirred at his presence (95, 9) ★ proclaim to the nations that the Lord has reigned (95, 10).

On the feast of the Ascension, however, and thereafter through the last Saturday after Pentecost add the following verses before saying the Glory be to the Father:

And he ascended into heaven ★ *and is seated at the right hand of the most holy Father in heaven.*

Be exalted above the heavens, O God ★ and your glory above all the earth (56, 12).

And we know that he is coming ★ coming to judge with justice (95, 13).

Second Office

Said daily, beginning on Holy Saturday at Compline and extending through the Octave of Pentecost including the Vespers on Saturday.

Psalm for Compline (Psalm 69):

37j.   Be mindful to assist me ★ make haste, O Lord, to help me.

Let them be abashed and dismayed ★ who are seeking my life.

Let them be routed and put to the blush ★ who wish me evil.

Let them quickly turn away blushing ★ who keep saying to me, Good for you!

But may all who seek you ★ exult and be

glad in you.

And may those ever say, The Lord be glorified, ★ who yearn for help from you.

But I am poor and resourceless ★ help me, O God.

You are my helper and deliverer ★ delay not, O Lord.

Psalm for Matins:

37k. Sing a new song to the Lord ★ for he has done marvelous things (97, 1).

His right hand and his holy arm (97, 1) ★ *have sanctified his Son.*

The Lord has made it known that he saves ★ he has revealed his justice for the nations to see (97, 2).

By day the Lord sent forth his mercy ★ and at night there is song for him (41, 9).

This is the day the Lord has made ★ let us rejoice and be glad at it (117, 24).

Blest is he who comes in the name of the Lord ★ the Lord is God and has given us light (117, 26-27).

Let the heavens rejoice, and the earth exult, and the sea be stirred and all that fills it ★ the fields shall be glad and everything in them (95, 11-12).

Bring to the Lord, you homes of the nations, bring honor and glory to the Lord ★ bring glory to the Lord for his name (95, 7-8).

From Ascension day on through the Octave of

Pentecost there are added here daily the following verses:

Kingdoms of the earth, sing to God, chant a hymn to the Lord (67, 33) ⋆ chant a hymn to God, who ascends the highest heaven over east (67, 34).

Lo, he will voice his words in a voice of power: "Give glory to God for Israel" ⋆ his might and magnificence ride in the clouds (67, 35).

Wondrous is God in his holy place. ⋆ The God of Israel will give might and strength to his people. Blest be God (67, 36).

From Easter Sunday to the feast of the Ascension one may say Psalm 29, "I will extol you, O Lord," instead of this psalm at Matins and at Vespers.

At the Prime:

The psalm "Have mercy on me" is said as at Prime **37e.**

At the Tierce, the Sext, and the None:

The psalm "Sing a new song" is said as at Matins **37k.**

At Vespers:

The psalm "Oh, clap your hands" is said as at Vespers **37i.**

But before the Glory be to the Father, add the verses indicated there to be said from Ascension day till Advent.

Third Office

For Sundays and the principal feasts (from Compline of the day preceding) beginning with Trinity Sunday and extending till the last Saturday before Advent; and again from the octave day of Epiphany excluded through holy Thursday.

Psalm for Compline:

Take Psalm 69, "Be mindful" as at Compline **37j.**

Psalm for Matins:

Take psalm "Sing a new song" as at Matins, **37k,** with the added verses assigned for Ascension day.

Psalm for the Prime:

Take psalm "Have mercy on me," as at the Prime **37e.**

Psalm for the Tierce:

37L. Cry jubilee to God, all the earth, sing a hymn to his name ★ give him glory and praise (65, 1-2).

Say to God, How terrifying are your works, O Lord ★ because of your teeming might your enemies pay false court to you (65, 3).

Let all the earth adore you and sing but to you ★ let it sing a hymn to your name (65, 4).

Come and hear, all you who fear God, and I will tell you ★ what great things he has done for my soul (65, 16).

With this voice of mine I cried out to him ★ with my tongue I gave glory to him (65, 17).

And from his holy temple he gave heed to my voice ⋆ and my alarm came before him (17, 7).

Oh, bless our God, you nations ⋆ and make the voice of his praise be heard (65, 8).

And all the tribes of the earth shall be blest in him ⋆ all the nations shall glorify him (71, 17).

Blest be the Lord, the God of Israel ⋆ for he alone does wondrous things (71, 18).

And blest forever be the name of his majesty ⋆ and all the earth shall be filled with his majesty. So be it, so be it (71, 19).

Psalm for the Sext:

37m. May the Lord hear you in the day of tribulation ⋆ may the name of the Lord of Jacob protect you (19, 2).

May he send you help from his sanctuary ⋆ and defend you from out of Sion (19, 3).

May he be mindful of all your sacrifices ⋆ and may your burnt-offering be rich in favor (19, 4).

May he grant you your heart's desire ⋆ and give approval to your every design (19, 5).

We shall rejoice at your rescuing us ⋆ and we shall be glorified in the name of the Lord our God (19, 6).

The Lord fulfil all your petitions ⋆ Now I know that the Lord has sent *his Son Jesus Christ* (19, 7) and he shall judge the nations with justice (9, 9).

And the Lord has become a refuge for the poor man, a helper when needed in troubles and trials ★ and let those who know your name put their hope in you (9, 10-11).

Blest be the Lord, my God (143, 1) ★ for you have proved my sustainer and my refuge in the day of my trouble (58, 17).

To you, my aid, will I sing ★ for you are God my sustainer, my God, and my mercy (58, 18).

Psalm for the None:

37n. In you, O Lord, I place my hope, let me not be put to shame ★ in your justice deliver and rescue me (70, 1-2).

Turn your ear to me ★ and save me (70, 2).

Be to me a God to protect me ★ and a fortified place to keep me safe (70, 3).

For you, O God, are my reliance ★ my hope, O Lord, from my youth (70, 5).

In you from birth have I had assurance, from my mother's womb have you been my protector ★ of you is my song forever (70, 6).

Let my mouth be full of praise to sing of your glory ★ all the day long of your grandeur (70, 8).

Hear my prayer, O Lord, for your mercy is tender ★ in your plentiful pitying mercy look down at me (68, 17).

And turn your face not away from your servant ★ in distress as I am, do hasten to hear me (68, 18).

Blest be the Lord my God (143, 1) ★ for you have proved my sustainer and my refuge in the day of my trouble (58, 17).

To you, my aid, will I sing ★ for you are my sustainer, my God, and my mercy (58, 18).

Psalm for the Vespers:

Take the psalm "Oh, clap your hands," as at Vespers 37i.

Fourth Office

Said daily from Compline on Saturday before the first Sunday of Advent through the None on Christmas eve.

Psalm for Compline (Psalm 12):

37o. How long, O Lord, will you altogether forget me ★ how long will you turn your face from me?

How long shall I have to worry in mind ★ bear grief in my heart all the day long?

How long shall my foe keep triumphing over me? ★ Look down at me, O Lord, my God, and hear my prayer.

Keep lighting my eyes lest some day I fall asleep in death ★ lest my foe should ever say, I have prevailed against him.

Those who beset me will exult if I am shaken ★ while I have been putting my trust in your mercy.

My heart will exult at your saving me ★ I

will sing of the Lord who has shown me favor, and chant praise to the name of the Lord most high.

Psalm for Matins:

37p. I will give thanks to you, O Lord, *most holy Father, King of Heaven and Earth* ⋆ because you have comforted me (85, 12 and 17).

You are my God and Savior (24, 5) ⋆ I will act with confidence and have no fear (Is. 12, 2).

The Lord is my strength and my glory ⋆ and he has proved my salvation (117, 14).

Your right hand, O Lord, has mightily shown its power, your right hand, O Lord, has struck the enemy ⋆ in your plenteous glory you have put down my adversaries (Ex. 15, 6-7).

Let the lowly look at it and be glad ⋆ seek ye God and your soul shall live (68, 33).

Let the heavens and the earth give praise ⋆ the sea too, and all things that move about in it (68, 35).

For God will rescue Sion ⋆ and the cities of Juda shall be rebuilt (68, 36).

And the people shall be at home in it ⋆ and acquire it as their heritage (68, 36).

And the seed of his servants shall possess it ⋆ and those who love his name shall abide in it (68, 37).

Psalm for the Prime:

Take psalm "Have mercy on me" as for the Prime **37e.**

Psalm for the Tierce:

Take psalm "Cry jubilee to God" as for the Tierce **37L.**

Psalm for the Sext:

Take psalm "May the Lord hear you" as for the Sext **37m.**

Psalm for the None:

Take psalm "In you, O Lord" as for the None **37n.**

Psalm for Vespers:

Take psalm "Oh, clap your hands" as at Vespers **37i.**

The psalm, however, is said only up to and including the verse "Make sacrifice of your person." "Let all the earth" and the rest of the psalm is not said.

Fifth Office

At Vespers on the eve of Christmas and *at all the Hours* from then on daily through the Vespers on the octave day of Epiphany, the following psalm is said:

37q. Exult in God, our helper (80, 2) ★ cry jubilee to the Lord, the true and living God, with a voice of exultation (46, 2).

For the Lord is high aloft and worthy of

awe ★ the great King over all the earth (46, 3).

For our most holy Father in Heaven, our King from of old, has sent his beloved Son from on high ★ and he has been born of the blessed Virgin Saint Mary.

He shall address me, You are my Father (88, 27) ★ and I will make him my first-born, high above all the kings of the earth (88, 28).

By day the Lord sent forth his mercy ★ and at night there is song for him (41, 9).

This is the day the Lord has made ★ let us rejoice and be glad at it (117, 24).

For the beloved most holy Child has been given to us and born for our sake at the wayside and laid in a manger ★ because he had no room in the inn.

Glory be to God the Lord in the highest ★ and on earth peace to people of good will (Lk. 2, 14).

Let the heavens rejoice, and the earth exult, and the sea be stirred, and all that fills it ★ the fields shall be glad and everything in them (95, 11-12).

Sing to him a new chant ★ sing, all the earth, to the Lord (95, 1).

For great is the Lord and greatly to be praised ★ he is worthy of awe above all gods (95, 4).

Bring to the Lord, you homes of the nations, bring honor and glory to the Lord ★ bring glory to the Lord for his name (95, 7-8).

Make sacrifice of your person and carry his holy cross ★ and follow his most holy precepts even to the end.

Part III

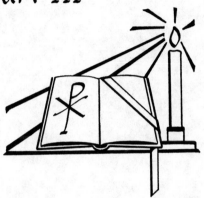

Saint Francis
Founds
A Way of Life

PART III

St. Francis founds a way of life

The ideals of St. Francis were safe, anchored so deeply in the love of God. God did not keep him waiting too long. About three years after his conversion, in 1209, there came to him one Bernard of Quintavalle. There was the following interchange:

38. Bernard: "If a person had certain goods of his lord in his possession for a long time and did not want to keep them any longer, what would be the more perfect thing to do about them?"

Francis: "Why, give them all up again to his lord."

Bernard: "Everything I have I recognize as given to me by God, and at your advice I stand here ready to give it up to him again."

Francis: "If you want to prove what you say with deeds, let us go to church early in the morning, and then let us take the Gospel book and seek advice of Christ."—2C 15.

In greater detail, at this point is LF 2:

"What you speak of, Bernard, is something

so great and wondrous that on it we ought to seek counsel from our Lord Jesus Christ and ask him to please show us his will in it and teach us how we can put it into practice. So, let us go together to the bishop's or to some good priest, and we will have him say Mass. Then we will remain in prayer till the Tierce, asking God to show us on a threefold opening of the Missal what it pleases him to have us choose."

39. On opening the book, the three first words were:

"If you wish to be perfect, go and sell everything you have, and give it to the poor."

"Take nothing with you on the way."

"Whoever wishes to follow me, let him deny himself."—2C 15.

Francis exclaimed:

"That is what I want, that is what I am looking for, that is what I long to do with all my inmost heart."—1C 22.

40. He turned to Bernard:

"That is the counsel Christ is giving us. Go, therefore, and do exactly what you have heard. And blest be the name of our Lord Jesus Christ, who has pointed out to us the way of the Gospel life."—LF 2.

With the thought in mind that our Lord praises the little, he declared:

41. "I want this brotherhood to be called the Order of the Lesser Brothers."—1C 38.

42. Not in any vague sense was it to be the Gospel life. What Francis meant by Gospel life, was clear from his very first rule:

"The rule and life of these brothers is this, namely to live in obedience, in chastity, and without property, and to follow the teaching and footsteps of our Lord Jesus Christ."— O p. 25, **283a.**

43. Obedience, he placed first, as he did also in the final rule of 1223, and in the rule of St. Clare. The very first words of the First Rule— and similarly of the Clare rule—stress the same specific obedience:

"Let Brother Francis, and whoever will be the head of this order, promise obedience and reverence to the Lord Pope Innocent III and his successors. And let the rest of the brothers be bound to obey Brother Francis and his successors."—O p. 24, **283.**

44. The first thought of Francis when he had eleven brothers about him, was of approval by the Pope:

"Brothers, I see that the Lord in his mercy means to increase our company. So, let us go to our mother, the holy Roman Church, and make known to the Pope what the Lord has begun to do through us so that we may carry

on with what we have begun, with his pleasure
and command."—LTC 12.

45. The stumbling-block to approval was the
total poverty singly and in common demanded
by the rule. Francis disarmed the Pope's misgiv-
ings that such total poverty would be tempting
Providence:

"A certain quite poor but fair lady lived in
a deserted countryside. A certain king fell in
love with her for her very great comeliness.
He was happy to marry her and be begot
most handsome sons of her. When they grew
up and had been nobly reared, their mother
said to them: 'Do not be ashamed at being
poor, my dears, for you all are children of
that great king. Go to his court with full confidence and ask him for whatever you need.'

"When they heard this they marveled and
were very happy. Encouraged by the pledge
of their royal parentage and knowing that
they were heirs-to-be, they looked on all
their indigence as wealth. They boldly presented themselves to the king and had no
dread of his countenance, whose resemblance
they bore.

"Recognizing his likeness in them, the king
in wonderment asked them whose children
they were. When they declared they were the
sons of the poor little lady in the wilds, the
king embraced them and said: 'My children
and heirs you are. Do not fear. For if even

strangers are fed at my table, it is the more fair that I have those fed there on whom all the inheritance entails by legal right.'

"So the king gave orders to the lady that all the sons he had begotten be sent to him and supported at his court."—2C 16.

46. The account goes on:

"My lord, I am that poor woman whom God loved and in his mercy so arrayed, by whom it pleased him to beget lawful children.

"The King of Kings has told me that he will provide for the children born of me, since if he feeds strangers, he ought in propriety also provide for his lawful children.

"For if the Lord gives worldly goods to sinners because of his love for his children who are in need of provision, much more will he be bounteous to people who live according to the Gospel, since to them it is due by right."—LTC 12; similarly B 3.

47. To Francis, being pledged to this Gospel life was high knighthood:

"Dearest brother, God has conferred a great favor on you. If the emperor were to come to Assisi and decide to make one of its citizens a knight or private chamberlain of his, would the offer not be welcomed as a great mark of honor and distinction? How much more should you rejoice since God has

called you to be his knight and his special servant to observe his holy Gospel perfectly."
—LF Life of Br. Giles.

48. It was to him a great responsibility:

"God has called us to this holy rule of life for the salvation of the world, and he has made this contract between us and the world: that we give a good example to the world, and the world in turn provide for our needs. So, let us continue to live in holy poverty, because that is the way of perfection, and the token and pledge of everlasting wealth."—LF. 2nd Stigm.

49. And a treasure:

"Let us go to St. Peter and St. Paul, and ask them to teach us and help us get possession of the measureless treasure of holy poverty; for it is a treasure so exceedingly valuable that we are unfit to hold it in the base vessels we are. It is that heavenly virtue by which all earthly transitory things are trodden under foot and every hindrance is removed from the soul, so that it can commune freely with the eternal God. It helps the soul while still on earth to converse with the angels in Heaven, it was the companion of Christ on the Cross, it was buried with Christ, it rose again with Christ, and with Christ it ascended into Heaven. It is the virtue, too, which renders their flight to Heaven easy for

those who love it. It protects us with the
armor of true humility and charity."—LF 13.
See **16.**

50. It has its earthly advantages:

"If we owned anything, we should have to
have weapons to protect ourselves. That is
what gives rise to contentions and lawsuits,
and so often causes the love of God and neighbor to be interfered with. For ourselves, we
are resolved to possess nothing temporal in
this world."—LTC 9.

51. Poverty to him meant simplicity, stripping
away all pretensions. He said of forthright
Brother Juniper:

"Would to God I had a vast forest full of
such junipers."—LF Life of Br. Juniper.

52. He said to a recruit:

"If you want to join the poor of God, first
distribute your goods to the poor."

When the man, instead, guilefully gave his
property to his kin:

"Go your way, brother fly*, because you
have not yet gone forth from your house and
your kindred. You gave your goods to your
relatives, defrauding the poor, and so you are
not worthy of a place with the holy poor. Beginning in the flesh, you have laid a ruinous
foundation for a spiritual structure."—2C 80.

53. The order was for the learned and un-learned, but both must put God first:

"God is no respecter of persons: and the minister general of this order, the Holy Ghost, alights on a poor and plain man just as on any other."—2C 193.

54. He illustrated that as follows:

"Suppose there were a general chapter of all the religious in the Church. Since therefore there are lettered and unlettered present, persons with knowledge and persons who lacking knowledge still know how to please God, one of the wise men and one of the plain men are assigned to preach. Wise as he is, the wise man deliberates and reasons thus: 'There is no place here for me to display my learning with men perfect in learning present, and it ill becomes me to make myself conspicuous for artistry while speaking about subtle matters among these highly subtle men. Perhaps it will be more beneficial to speak simply.'

"The appointed day comes, the assemblies of the saints foregather, athirst to hear the sermon. The wise man steps forth dressed in sackcloth and with ashes sprinkled on his head. To the admiration of everybody, preaching rather by his action, he cuts his words short, saying:

" 'Great things have we promised, greater are promised to us.

The former let us observe, to the latter let
us aspire.

Brief is the pleasure, eternal the penalty.

Slight is the suffering, the glory is measureless.

Many are called, few are chosen, all have
their requital.'

"Their hearts crushed, the hearers burst
into tears and venerate the truly wise man
like a saint.

" 'Such luck!' says the plain man in his
heart. 'The wise man has gotten in ahead of
me with everything I meant to do or say. But I
know what I will do: I know some Psalm
verses. I will act the wise man's role, since the
latter has acted the role of the plain man.' The
next day's session comes, the plain man arises
and gives out a psalm as his theme. So,
touched by the breath of the Spirit of God, he
proceeds to discourse by God's inspired gift
so fervently, so subtly, so sweetly that full of
amazement all actually say, 'With the simple
is his communication.' "

The man of God thus explained this moral
parable:

"Our order is a very great company and so
to say a general synod, coming together from
every part of the world under a single pattern
of life. In it the wise for their benefit take over
what is proper to the plain, when they find the

unlettered pursuing heavenly aims with fiery energy and people untaught by men growing wise in spiritual matters through the Spirit. In it likewise the plain convert to their profit what is proper to the wise, when they see distinguished men who could have a glorious life anywhere in the world, humbly stooping to the same practices with themselves. That is where the beauty of this blessed family shines forth, the manifold garnishments of which afford no little pleasure to the Head of the family."—2C 191, 192.

55. His thought on learning is clear from the charge he gave St. Anthony*:

"To Brother Anthony, my bishop, Brother Francis gives greeting: It is agreeable to me to have you read sacred Theology to the brothers, so long as over this study they do not extinguish the spirit of prayer and devotion, as is contained in the rule."—Chronicle of the 24 Generals.

56. Francis once said that a great cleric ought in a way to bid farewell even to his learning when he came to the order, so that expropriating a possession such as that he could offer himself stripped to the embrace of Christ:

"Learning renders many persons indocile, not permitting them to unbend under humble observances from a certain setness of theirs. So I should like to see a lettered man first make this request to me: 'See, brother, I have lived a long time in the world and yet have not learned to know God truly. I beg you, grant me a spot removed from the noise of the world where I can think over my past years in sorrow, and where by collecting my scattered forces I can reshape my spirit for better things.'

"What do you think a man beginning like that would come to be? He would really go about everything with the vigor of an unchained lion, and the blessed energy he drank in at the start would develop in him by steady stages. You could in time safely give him over to a genuine ministry of the word, for he would begin pouring out the force aboil in him."—2C 194.

57. It grieved Francis to see learning pursued where virtue was neglected. He said:

"My brothers who are led by curious craving for knowledge, will find their hands empty on the day of retribution. I would rather have them growing strong in virtue, that when the periods of tribulation came they could have the Lord with them in their distress. For tribulation is going to come, such that, useless for any purpose, their books will be flung out of windows and into cubby-holes."— 2C 195.

58. His thought on learning is further illustrated by such sayings as the following:

"Emperor Charles, Roland, Oliver and all the paladins and stalwarts who were mighty in battle, pursuing the infidels with much sweat and toil, even to death, achieved a memorable victory over them and finally they died in battle for the Faith of Christ. Now, however, there are many who would like to receive honor and praise for only telling what they did. So there are many among us too, who for merely repeating and preaching about what the saints did want to enjoy honor and praise."—MP 4.

59. On another occasion:
"There are so many eager for the climb to knowledge that the man is blessed who keeps himself barren of it for the love of God."—MP 4.

60. "A man has only as much knowledge as he puts into action, and a religious is only as good a preacher as he puts into action. For the tree is known only by its fruits."—MP 4.

61. On the other hand, as to learned brothers studying the Scriptures, in which he himself was deeply versed:
"Of course it pleases me, provided that after the example of Christ, of whom we read that he prayed rather than read, they do not neglect the pursuit of prayer and that they study it in order not only to learn how to

preach, but to put what they hear into practice, and then when they have practiced it, let them set it down for others to practice.

"I wish my brothers to be Gospel students and to advance in knowledge of the truth in a way that they likewise grow in unspoiled simplicity, so that they do not separate the simplicity of the dove from the wisdom of the serpent, for our excellent Master linked the two in his blest mouth."—B 11.

61a. Of priests and theologians he said:

"And all the theologians and persons who administer the most holy words of God, we must honor and respect as people who minister spirit and life to us."—**282b.**

62. In nothing was Francis so set in the new way of life as on respect for Mother Church in the person of Pope, Bishop, and Priest. Thus his way not not only differed from movements common in his day, but they leave no ground for any attempt such as has been made in our times, to make of him a rebel against the Church. Cf. title Church in our Topical Index.

He sought the approval of the Pope for his first rule in 1209. He went again and again to the Pope: to ask for the Portiuncula indulgence; to secure a Cardinal Protector; to get the approval of his final rule Nov. 29, 1223; at which time he likewise sought approval for his Crib at Greccio (Christmas 1223). His rules, all his Testament, all authenticated actions and sayings of his stress submissiveness and respect for pope, bishop, priest. He spent hours, even days, with Cardinal Ugolino, the later Pope Gregory IX, in Rome and elsewhere. The dates cover every period of his life, no period more so than the critical last six years of his life. Pope, Bishop, Priest—they meant everything to him in the new way of life, for they meant the Gospel, the Faith, the Church, Christ to him, and without these latter nothing meant anything to him.

Such passages as the following, added to instances cited above, illustrate his attitude:

"From the beginning of my conversion the Lord put his word in the mouth of the bishop of Assisi, so that he gave me good advice and fortified me in the service of Christ. For that reason and many other excellent considerations which I find with regard to prelates, I want to love, honor and take as my masters not only the bishops but also any poor insignificant priests."—MP 10.

63. "If I were at the same time to meet some saint coming down from Heaven and any poor little priest, I would first pay my respects to the priest and proceed to kiss his hands first. I would say, 'Ah, just a moment, St. Lawrence, because this person's hands handle the Word of Life and possess something that is more than human.' "—2C 201.

64. "These hands have touched my Lord, and no matter what they be like, they could not soil Him or lessen His virtue. To honor the Lord, honor his minister. He can be bad for himself, but for me he is good" . . . of a priest accused to him of a sinful life.—SdB.

He would have recourse to them even if they persecuted him (**282a**).

65. Typical was his request for the Portiuncula Indulgence:

"Holy Father, if it please your Holiness, I wish that because of the blessings God has bestowed and will still bestow in this place, all who come here truly contrite and confessed may have a plenary indulgence of all their sins, so that they will have no further score to pay."—TJC.

"For how many years?"

"Holy Father, may it please your Holiness to grant not years but souls—non annos sed animas."

Then, when the Holy Father rebuked him for not requesting a document:

"Your word is enough for me. If it is the work of God, it is for him to make his own work known. I desire to have no other document for it, but the Blessed Virgin Mary alone shall be my document. Amen."—LTC 19.

66. Concluding the words of St. Francis, for the moment, on the new way of life he founded, we may add how he further treasured the Portiuncula:

"My sons, see to it that you never abandon this place. Should you be driven out one way, come back another way. For this place is truly holy and God's abode. Here, when we were few, the Most High increased us. Here he enlightened the hearts of his poor with the light of wisdom, and here he inflamed our wills with the fire of his love. Whoever prays here with a heart full of devotion will obtain what he is asking, but who offends here will be the more heavily punished. Therefore, my sons, regard this place of God's dwelling as worthy of all honor, and with all your heart, with a voice of exultation and praise, give thanks there to God."—1C 106.

67. It was to be the model for the rest of the order:

"This place is a model and pattern for the entire order, and I would rather have the brothers of this place put up with hardships and inconveniences for love of the Lord God here and have the rest of the brothers who come here carry its good example of poverty back to their places rather than that those here should have comforts in full measure and the rest take it as the building pattern for their places, saying: In the place of St. Mary of the Portiuncula, the main place of our order, they

put up buildings of such size and kind; so we
too can well build at our places."—MP 8.

67a. And we may add how he foresaw his way
of life extended to the devout sex:

"Come and help me with the work at St.
Damian's church, for it will be a convent of
ladies whose good name and life will glorify
our Heavenly Father all over the Church."—
LTC 7.

Part IV

Saint Francis
Addresses himself
to Virtue

PART IV

St. Francis addresses himself to virtue

68. No one ever took more seriously than St. Francis the propriety of practicing virtue before undertaking to teach it. It would be far easier to demonstrate that with what he did than with what he said, as we have undertaken to do.

Let us begin with his remarkable tribute entitled:

SALUTE TO THE VIRTUES

"Hail, Queen Wisdom! The Lord save you,
　　with your holy sister pure Simplicity.
Holy Lady Poverty, the Lord save you,
　　with your sister holy Humility.
Holy Lady Charity, the Lord save you,
　　with your sister holy Obedience.
All you most holy virtues, may the Lord
　　save you,
　　for from him do you proceed and
　　come to us.

"No one there is in all the world
　　that can possess any one among you
　　unless first he die.*

Whoever has one of you,
and does not offend the rest,
has all of you.
And whoever offends against any one of
you, has none and offends against you all.

"And every one of you puts vice and sin to
rout:
Holy wisdom shames the Devil and all his
evil arts;
Holy pure simplicity shames all the wisdom
of this world, and the wisdom of the flesh.
Holy poverty shames all grasping and
hoarding, and the worries of this world.
Holy humility gives shame to pride
and anybody of this world,
and anything in all the world.
Holy charity gives shame to all temptations
of the Devil, and the flesh, and any
carnal fear.
Holy obedience shames all self-will of flesh
and body, and keeps a body mortified to
obey the spirit, and obey one's fellow
man.
It makes a person subject to anybody in
this world; and not to men alone, but to
all the beasts and wild things, so that
they can do what they please with him
so far as the Lord on high might grant
it them."—O 20.

69. *The love of God*—the holy wisdom he praises above—dominated his life. To him it was a sacred thing:

"The love of God is something so sublime and precious it ought never to be mentioned except rarely and under great necessity, and with much reverence."—MP 34.

70. Again and again there is in his writings the plea to pick up stray writing lest the name of God be there*. Asked why he wanted even pagan writings picked up, he said:

"Because the letters are there which spell the glorious name of God our Lord. The good, too, which is in them, does not belong to the pagans nor to any other human beings, but to God alone, who is all that is good."—1C 82.

71. Elsewhere in these pages we carry examples of his prayers (cf. title Prayer in our Topical Index). It remains to say that at prayer he wanted composure:

"If the body takes its food while at rest, yet both food and body are to be eaten by worms; with what peace and composure ought the soul to take its food, which is God!" 2C 96.

72. A bowl he was carving, later distracted him at prayer; he threw it into the fire:

"Bah, the silly gimcrack! To have power enough over me to distract my mind toward it! I will sacrifice it to the Lord, with whose sacrifice it has interfered . . . Shame on us for being rapt away to these trivial fancies when at prayer time we are addressing the Great King."—2C 97.

73. He was miserly about one thing: consolations at prayer.

"When a servant of God is visited by the Lord with some fresh consolation while at prayer, before leaving his prayers he ought to raise his eyes to heaven and say to the Lord with folded hands: You have, O Lord, sent unworthy sinful me this consolation and sweetness from Heaven, and I commit it back to you to save it for me, for I am a thief when it comes to your treasure . . . Lord, take your good gift from me in this world, and save it for me in the world to come.

"That is what he ought to do; so that when he comes away from prayer, he will appear to others as much a poor sinful person as if he had not gained any further grace . . . It happens that an invaluable thing is lost at a cheap price; and that easily provokes the Giver not to give another time."—2C 99.

74. He used to see God in everything; also in his fellow man, rich or poor. Of the rich he said:

"God is the Lord over them as well as over us. He can call them to his service and justify them when called. . . . They are our brothers, because they have the same Creator as we; and our masters, because they lend their help so that the good can pursue penance with them supplying their bodily needs."—LTC 14.

75. As to the poor:

"Whoever says anything evil to a poor man, insults Christ by it, for the poor man bears the mark of Christ's nobility, who made himself poor for us in this world."—1C 76.

76. To a companion who had prejudged a poor man's motives:

"Now hurry up, take off your habit, get down on your knees to this poor man, and declare yourself at fault. And do not only beg his pardon, but beseech him for his prayers. . . .

"When you see a poor man, brother, a mirror of the Lord and his poor Mother is held up to you!

"In like manner consider in the sick the infirmities he took upon himself."—2C 85.

77. "When you see a poor person, you ought to consider Him in whose name he comes, Christ that is, who took our poverty and infirmity on himself. For such a person's infirmity and poverty is a kind of mirror for us, in which we ought to behold with pitying regard the infirmity and poverty which our Lord Jesus Christ bore in his person for our sake."—MP 37.

78. His own poverty he must not mind, because:

"If we were well covered within with flaming love for our home in Heaven, we might easily bear the cold from without."—B 5.

79. In love with God's love for us was he:

"Well deserving of our love is the love of Him who loved us so well."—2C 196.
See also his prayer *Absorbeat*, **33.**

80. He loved that love in holy Mass, in the churches*. But when he could not be present:

"When I do not hear Mass, I adore the body of our Christ with the eyes of the mind in prayer, just as I adore it when I see it at Mass."—BSF.

81. At Elevation he would say:

"O Lord God, Father in Heaven, look on the glorious countenance of your Christ, and have mercy on me and all other sinners, for whom your blest Son, our Lord, has deigned to die and for whose salvation and consolation he wished to remain with us in the holy Sacrament of the Altar. With Him you are, O Father, and the Holy Ghost, you who are one God and live with Son and Holy Ghost world without end. Amen."—Opera Omnia S.P.N.F., Wadding-de la Haye, p. 18.

82. Crib, Cross, Altar! The cross is to come

for Francis. The Crib was a favorite with him. He said jestingly:

"When I have speech with the emperor, I will beseech him to have a general ordinance issued that all who can afford it shall strew wheat and other grain along the roads, so that the little birds, especially our sister larks, may have an abundance on so solemn a feast day."
—2C 200.

MP 114 goes on:

. . . "and that out of reverence for the Son of God, whom on that night the Blessed Virgin Mary laid down in a manger between ox and ass, whoever has an ox and an ass shall on that night supply them with the best of good feed; that likewise on that day all the poor ought to be given their fill of good victuals by the rich."

83. "With the Lord born for us, it has become a matter of propriety for us to save ourselves—oportuit nos salvari."—MP 114.

In other words, shame on us if we do not!

84. "Brother, it is sinful of you to call the day Friday on which the Child has been born for us. I would like even the walls to eat meat on a day like that, and since they cannot, to be rubbed with it outwardly."—2C 199.

85. Eternally memorable is the Christmas at Greccio celebrated in 1223, after Francis had gone to Rome for the approval of the final rule. He sent word to Sir John Velita:

"If you wish us to celebrate the festival of our Lord at Greccio, hurry on ahead and prepare exactly what I am telling you. For I want to observe the memory of that Child who was born at Bethlehem, and in some way see before my bodily eyes the discomforts of his baby needs, how he was laid there in the manger, and how, with the ox and the ass standing by, he was placed there on the hay." —1C 84.

People were to come with candles and torches, at midnight; a crib like our Savior's at Bethlehem was to be made ready so that it held the altar stone on which the Sacred Species were to rest at Consecration. Francis preached, but he could not say "Jesus," but only "the Babe of Bethlehem," bleating the "Bethlehem" like a sheep.

86. Of other devotions, we have seen and shall see how St. Francis loved the Blessed Trinity, Mary, the blessed Mother, loved the angels and saints.* Of the angels, he fasted a lent in honor of St. Michael, saying:

"Everybody ought to offer God something by way of praise or of special gift to honor so great a prince."—2C 197.

He received the Stigmata in the Michaelmas fast of 1224.

87. Of St. Peter and St. Paul he hoped to get

the grace of poverty 49. Of St. Peter especially, he said on his earliest visit to Rome:

"The Prince of Apostles should in fairness be honored magnificently. Why then do these people make such skimpy offerings in the church where his body rests?"—LTC 3.

88. Seeing God in things meant seeing himself as God saw him, hence his deep *humility:*
"What a man is in the eyes of God, so much he is, and no more."—B 6.

89. "Just as in a picture of our Lord or the Blessed Virgin painted on wood our Lord and the Blessed Virgin are honored and yet the wood and the painting ascribe nothing of it to themselves, so is the servant of God a kind of painting of God in which God is honored for his benefaction, but the servant ought to attribute nothing to himself, because in comparison with God he is even less than wood or painting, indeed he is pure nothing.

"So, to God alone the honor and glory should be given, to himself however nothing but shame and tribulation so long as he lives in this world."—MP 45.

90. When the bishop of Terni introduced him to his people as a poor, insignificant, illiterate man through whom God was doing wonders, Francis was entranced with happiness:

"Frankly, my lord bishop, you have done me great honor today, for while others take my dues from me, you are one who has kept them as they belong. Like a discerning man, I say, you have kept the valuable apart from the valueless, by ascribing the praise to God, the insignificant to me."—2C 141.

91. Similarly when Brother Masseo teasingly asked him why all the world must flock to him:

"Do you want to know why everybody is following me? That is happening to me because of the eyes of God on high taking in everywhere the good and the bad. Those most holy eyes have espied nobody among sinners more useless, incompetent, and sinful than me, and to do the marvels he has in mind, he has found no more worthless creature on earth. And so he has chosen me, to put to shame what is noble and grand and powerful and fair and wise about the world, so that it may be clear that all virtue and all that is good comes from him and not from any creature; and no person may glory in his sight, but whoever glories, shall glory in the Lord, to whom be all the honor and glory forever."—LF 10.

92. "To myself I seem to be the greatest of sinners, for if God had pursued a criminal with the same mercy, the man would be ten times more spiritual than I."—2C 123.

93. "Had the Most High bestowed as

much on a bandit, he would be more grateful than you are, Francis."—2C 133.

94. Always he was conscious of his need of grace:

"I may have sons and daughters yet! Do not praise me as if I were safe. Nobody should be praised while his end is uncertain. Whenever it may suit the Giver to take away from me what he has lent me, only body and soul will remain, and even an infidel possesses them."—2C 133.

95. "Nobody ought to flatter himself with undue applause over anything that a sinner can do. A sinner can fast, pray, weep, mortify his flesh. But this he cannot do: remain loyal to his Lord. Therefore there is something to glory about if we render God his glory, if while serving him faithfully we ascribe to him whatever he gives us. The flesh is a man's greatest enemy: it has neither aftersight to be sorry for anything, nor foresight to be in fear of anything. Its one aim is to abuse the present. But what is worse, it claims for itself and credits to its glory what has fallen due not to it but to the soul. It plucks the praise for any virtues, the public favor for any vigils and prayers. It leaves the soul nothing, yes takes its toll even of any tears."—2C 134.

96. To offset the praise given him, he had a brother insult him:

"I order you under obedience to abuse me with hard words and to tell the truth to offset the falsehoods of these people."

And when the brother did his best:

"The Lord bless you, for what you say is very true. Such are the things the son of Peter Bernardone deserves to hear."—1C 53.

97. How different this Francis from the Francis who fairly whimpered, earlier, under his father's abuse, and engaged a poor man to bless him each time:

"Come with me, and I will give you some of the alms given me. Only, when you see my father curse me, I will say to you, 'Bless me, my father,' and then you make the sign of the Cross over me and bless me instead."—LTC 7.

98. Hence his great willingness to suffer:

"O my Lord Jesus Christ, I thank you for the great love you have shown me. For it is a token of great love if the Lord punishes his servant well for his faults in this life so that he may not be punished in the next."—LF 1st Stigm.

98a. Hence his *sincerity*. Due to his illness he needed certain indulgences, but the world must know of them. He was urged to wear a patch of fox pelt over his stomach inside his habit:

"If you want me to allow that under the tunic, then see that a patch of the same size is put on for me outside too, so that sewed on there it will indicate to people the fur patch hidden beneath."—2C 130.

98b. "You take me for a holy man, and so in your piety you have come here to me. But I want you to know that all this" (All Saints) "lent I have been eating food prepared with lard" (not otherwise permitted on fast days then).—2C 131.

99. "See here, look at this glutton, fattened on the meat of the chickens he ate unknown to you."—1C 52.

100. "It is not fitting that the people take me for an abstemious man while on the contrary I take meat for refreshment in secret."—B 6.

101. From the same motive of humble self-distrust he was scrupulously *chaste*. He would take no chance in favor of his weakness, against God's grace:

"I admit to you truthfully, brother, if I looked at (women), I should recognize none of them by their face but two. The features of so-and-so and so-and-so are known to me, but no one's else."—2C 112.

102. He could be cruel to himself to make his body head right in temptation. As he scourged himself:

"There now, brother Ass, that is the proper state for you, put under the lash that way! The habit is there to serve a religious life, it is a token of holiness, no lustful fellow has a right to steal it. If you are going to go any-where, go there!"—B 5.

103. Another time, leaping naked into a snow-drift and leisurely making snow figures there:

"See, this largest heap is your wife, these four are your two sons and two daughters, the other two are your man and your maid servant, whom you need to wait on you. Now hurry and dress them, they are dying of the cold. But if that manifold worry over them bothers you, then be in earnest and serve God alone."—B 5.

104. He was of course the world's greatest lover of *poverty*—in its total sense, of the gift of self as well as goods. A few passages may illus-trate further what is said elsewhere*:

"Since you have called this Francis's cell, setting it down as my property, find another dweller for it, for I will not stay in it any more. When the Lord was hemmed about where he prayed and fasted for forty days, he had no cell made for himself, nor any house, but just stayed under the crag of a mountain. We can follow him in the way he traced thus by having nothing of our own, though we cannot live without making use of houses."—2C 59.

104a. He frequently quoted our Lord's words (Mt. 8, 20) in pity and emulation:

"The foxes have their holes and the birds of the air their nests, but the Son of Man has no place to lay his head."—B 7.

105. Alms collected after honest work were treasure to him:

"Whoever gives me a piece worth a single sou, I can match him for it with a thousand gold marks; for when a servant of God asks for alms, he offers the love of God to those whom he asks, and compared with that everything there is in heaven and on earth is nothing."—MP 22.

106. "I want my brothers who are and who shall be, to know that I take greater comfort of soul and body when I sit at the wretched table of the brothers and see before me those miserable alms begged from door to door for the love of God, than when I sit at your table," Lord Cardinal, "and that of other lords, abundantly supplied as they are with such varied dishes. For the bread of alms is holy bread, hallowed by the love and praise of God, since whenever a brother goes out for alms, he has first to say, 'Praised and blest be God our Lord', and then, 'Give us an alms for the love of our Lord God'."—MP 23.

107. Nothing shamed him like a person **poorer** than himself:

"Brother, we must give this mantle back to this poor fellow, to whom it belongs. We had it as a loan until we might find someone poorer than ourselves." (Of course it was Francis's own mantle, but he would have it so:) "I don't want to be a thief, and it would be charged against us as theft if we did not give it to a needier person."—2C 87.

108. "I give you this cloak for the love of God on the condition that you give it up to nobody unless he pays you well for it."

. . . to a bereaved poor man, who then held on to it against the brothers themselves until he was compensated.—2C 88.

109. Part of poverty to him was *obedience*, the forfeiture of his independence for the love of God:

"Among other favors the Divine mercy has deigned to grant me, he bestowed this grace that I would obey a novice of an hour's standing if he were given me as my guardian as exactly as I would anybody else however aged and discerning. A subject ought to consider in his superior not the human person but Him for whose love he is subject. The more insignificant the one who presides, the more acceptable the humility of the person who obeys."—2C 151.

110. From the earliest days, head though he was, he preferred to follow another's lead. On the way to Rome to have the very first rule approved, he picked Brother Bernard to act as Pope:

"Let us make one of our number our leader and take him as the Vicar of Jesus Christ, and then we will go where he goes, and where he puts up, we will put up."—LTC 12.

111. When he abdicated, and Peter Cattaneo took his place as head of the order, he begged Brother Peter:

"I ask you for the love of God to commit your place over me to one of my associates, to whom I am to give the devoted obedience I give you. I know what the blessing of obedience is, and that none of the person's time passes without gain who has put his neck under the yoke of another."—2C 151.

112. "There is no prelate in all the world who is feared as much as the Lord would make me feared by my brothers if I desired it. But the Lord has granted me this grace that I wish to be contented with everything, like the least member in the order."—MP 46.

Part V

Saint Francis
Is Considerate

PART V

St. Francis is considerate

Seeing God in others, how could Francis be other than considerate of them—his brothers, the Poor Ladies of St. Clare, anybody whose path he crossed or who crossed his path.

113. He used to say:

"Courtesy is one of the properties of the Lord, who serves out sun and rain and all his things which we need for our life, to the just and the unjust alike. For Courtesy is a sister of Charity, and she extinguishes hatred and keeps Charity alive."—Legenda Antiqua.

114. There was the vocation of Brother John the Simple. John took a great liking to Francis and wanted to follow him. He was told, as usual, to give what he had to the poor. John felt he had worked hard enough to own one of the oxen of the family; he was ready to give it away. But the family, really in need, made a great outcry over man and ox. Francis got the picture:

"See, this son of yours wishes to serve God. You ought not to be sad about that but very glad. For not only as God regards it, but also as the world looks at it, credit is given you for

93

great honor and benefit to souls and bodies,
that God is honored of your flesh; and, too,
all our brothers will be your brothers. Because
he is a creature of God and wants to serve his
Creator, to serve whom is to reign, I neither
can nor ought to give him back to you. But so
that you have some comfort of him, it is my
will that he give up his right to the ox in your
favor as poor people, though according to the
Gospel he ought to give it to other poor."—
MP 57.

"So, calm your emotions! Look, I give back
the ox to you, you give me the brother."—
2C 190.

115. Orlando of Chiusi wanted Francis's advice. But when Francis met him, Orlando was
being entertained. To relieve both guests and host
of embarrassment, Francis said to Orlando:

"I shall be pleased to help. But go now,
visit with your friends who have invited you
to dinner and dine with them. After dinner
we will talk it over as long as you wish."—
LF 1st Stigm.

In appreciation Orlando presented the brothers
with La Verna, the later mount of the Stigmata.

116. Francis forgot no courtesy, even on his
deathbed:

"You know how loyal and devoted the
Lady Giacoma of Settesoli has been and is to
me and to our order. So I believe she will take

it as a great favor and comfort if you let her
know about my condition, and in particular if
you give her word to send me some ash-
colored habit cloth and with the cloth also
some of that confection she made for me on
occasion in Rome."—MP.

117. The Wadding-de la Haye edition of St.
Francis's works carries the note (Letter XVII) the
saint is supposed to have sent Lady Giacoma on
the subject. The spirit is there, if not the fact:

"To the Lady Giacoma, servant of the
Most High, Brother Francis, Jesus Christ's
poor little one, wishes greeting and the company of the Holy Ghost in the Lord Jesus
Christ:

"Know, very dear sister, that Christ the
blest in his mercy has revealed to me that
soon the end of my life will be at hand. So,
if you wish to find me alive, on seeing this
note hasten to come to St. Mary of the
Angels. If you come after Saturday you can
no longer find me living. And bring with you
some cloth or a hairshirt in which to wrap
my body, also wax for the burial services.
And I ask you to bring some of those confec-
tions you used to bring me when I lay ill in
Rome."

118. But the Lady Giacoma, due to presenti-
ment, anticipated the message:

"Blest be God, who has directed our

brother" (so he called the Lady) "Lady Giacoma to come to us. Open the doors and escort her in, for the ordinance regarding women need not be observed in the case of Brother Giacoma."—TRM 37.

119. Similar was his thought then of Lady Clare and her daughters:

"Go and tell the Lady Clare to put away all grief and sadness because she cannot see me just now. She shall know for certain that before her death both she and her sisters will see me and be greatly consoled in my behalf." —MP 108.

120. Indeed he never forgot Clare's generous gift of herself and her sisters to the Gospel life:

"Do not think, brothers, that I do not love them perfectly. If it were wrong to keep them devoted to Christ, was it not more so ever to betroth them to Christ? Really there would have been no harm in not calling them, but to be unconcerned about them now that they are called, were the worst sort of unkindness.

"But I am giving you an example that you may act as I do. I will not have anybody of his own accord offer to visit them. It is my wish that the most unwilling and reluctant be appointed to their service, spiritual men, approved by their worthy, long-standing good conduct."—2C 205.

121. St. Clare herself incorporated in the approved rule of her order these words of St. Francis:

"Because at Divine inspiration you have made yourselves daughters and servants of the most high sovereign King, our Father in Heaven, and have espoused yourselves to the Holy Ghost in choosing to live according to the perfection of the Holy Gospel, I purpose and promise that personally and through my brothers I will always give you the same attentive care and special concern as to them."—O 75.

122. His last will to St. Clare was:

"I, poor little Brother Francis, wish to follow the life and poverty of our most high Lord Jesus Christ and his most holy Mother, and to persevere therein to the last. And I beg you, my ladies, and give you the counsel to go on living in this most holy life and poverty. And be very much on your guard lest on anybody's instruction or advice you ever in any way depart from it."

123. Naturally, there was no less thoughtfulness for his own. Some of them needed consideration more than others. There was worried Brother Bernard:

"The first brother the Lord gave me was Brother Bernard. He was the first to take up and put in practice in the fullest way the perfection of the Holy Gospel by distributing

all his goods to the poor. For that reason and for many other favors I am bound to love him more than any other brother in all the order. So, it is my will and I ordain as far as I can that whoever is minister general, shall love and honor him as myself. The ministers too and all the brothers of the whole order shall regard him as being in my stead."
—MP 107.

124. He told of what was troubling Bernard:

"I tell you, to try him Brother Bernard has had the shrewdest devils, the more wicked among the rest of the spirits, put on him. But though they are always alert with their effort to make that star fall from heaven, the outcome will be otherwise. He will be plagued, goaded, afflicted, but at last he will enjoy wondrous calm and peace, and, his course finished, he will pass on to Christ."—2C 48.

125. Brother Leo was his faithful secretary and his confessor. Francis read his thoughts. There was a note from Francis to Leo one day, with the style of address reversed:

"Brother Leo, wish your Brother Francis health and peace!

"I tell you yes, my son! And like a mother! Everything we spoke about on the road, I dispose of with this sole word of advice. And if hereafter you need to come to me for advice, this is what I advise you: Whatever the way you believe you will best please the Lord

God and pursue his footsteps and his poverty, just take that way with the Lord's blessing and under my obedience. And if it is necessary for you for the good of your soul or some other personal consolation, and you, Leo, wish to come to me, just come!—O 116.

Other instances of consideration for Brother Leo see in **34** and **35**.

126. Brother Richer worried over his acceptability:

"Son, let no temptation disturb you, no brooding embitter you, because you are very dear to me. Know that among those especially dear to me, you deserve affection and close friendship. Feel at ease to call on me whenever you wish and make use of our friendship to speak freely."—1C 50.

127. Then there was the brother who overdid it in fasting and roused the community that night with cries about starving. Francis had all the brothers get up and sit at table with him lest he be embarrassed. He explained:

"What I did here about eating, was done purposely, not by inclination. Fraternal charity called for it. Let the charity, not the eating, be the lesson to you; for while the eating caters to gluttony, the charity caters to the spirit."—2C 22.

128. "Each of you should have regard for his own nature. Though this or that one may be able to sustain himself on less food than some one else, still I will not have him who needs more food try to imitate the former in that. Taking his own nature into consideration, let him bestow on his body what it needs in order to be able to serve the spirit.

"Just as we are bound to avoid superfluity in eating, for it harms body and soul, so must we beware of excessive abstaining, yes even more so, because the Lord wants mercy and not sacrifice.—MP 27.

129. "Brother body should be provided for discreetly, lest the heavy weather of listlessness loom up in that quarter. So that he does not tire of staying awake and persisting reverently in prayer, occasion for any murmuring should be removed. Else he would say, 'I am famishing and cannot bear the burden of your exertion!' If however after he had devoured fodder enough he were still to mutter such things, realize that as a lazy draft animal he needs the spurs; the goad is the thing for the slothful ass."—2C 129.

130. He never evaded the urgency of *good example* to the rest:

"If I should speak with the tongues of men and angels and have no charity in me, not giving my neighbor the example of virtue, I am of little service to him and of none to myself."—B 9.

131. "It is for me to be the model and pattern for all the brothers, and therefore although my body may need to wear a tunic with linings, still I must take the rest of my brothers into consideration who need the same thing and yet perhaps do not and cannot have it. So I must put myself in their place and suffer the same needs they bear, so that seeing me behave thus, they can bear up more patiently."—MP 16.

132. "The brothers do not have in mind that I could do with indulgent pity for my body. And so, because it is for me to be the pattern and example of all the brothers, I wish to have for my use and to be content with little and common food, and to use everything else as poverty requires, with utter loathing of what is delicate and expensive." —MP 27.

133. Offered a special permanent companion, he declined:

"I do not want to appear exceptional by using this privilege of free choice but let brothers from place to place go along with me as the Lord will inspire them. I once saw a blind man with no more than a little pup for a guide along the way."—2C 144.

134. Was God punishing him this time for overlooking the duty of example?

"The demons are our Lord's bailiffs, meant by him to punish misdemeanors. But it is a token of the greater favor of God if he leaves nothing unpunished about his servant while the latter is living in this world.

"Now, I recall no offense which by God's mercy I have not washed off by making satisfaction, because in his fatherly condescension he has always dealt with me so as to show me in prayer and meditation what pleased or displeased him.

"But maybe he has permitted his deputies to break in on me because my putting up at the court of notables does not look so proper . . . When my brothers who live in such poor places hear of my associating with cardinals, they will perhaps suspect that I am abounding in delights.

"So, brother, I deem it better for a man set up as an example, to shun courts and fortify those who are enduring the pinch of poverty by enduring something similar."— 2C 120.

135. He was sensitive to a fault about advantages over others, even in his illness. He read the mind of Brother Leonard of Assisi:

"No, brother, it is not right for me to be riding donkey-back while you go on foot. Out in the world you were of nobler, mightier rank that I."—2C 31.

136. "I have never been a robber in the

matter of alms to the extent of getting or using them beyond need. I have always taken less than was due to me for fear other poor people be cheated of their portion. To do otherwise would be robbery."—MP 12.

137. He spared a returning deserter early confrontation. The brothers marveled:

"Why wonder at my keeping out of his sight? You do not see the reason: I took recourse to prayer, to deliver him from his wrong notions. I was rightly displeased in what I saw in him as my son, but now, by the grace of my Christ, all his delusion has vanished."

Later, to the brother:

"God pardon you, brother. But take care in future lest under the pretext of holiness you let yourself be at variance with the order and your brothers."—2C 33.

138. Sensitive about the feelings of lepers, he called them *brother Christians*, meaning Christ followers in a special way. When a simple brother led some of them as his charges out among a squeamish public:

"You should not lead these *brother Christians* about in that way: it is not proper, neither for you, nor for them."

On second thought, however, he believed that must look like discrimination:

"Let this be my penance that I eat from

the same dish with my brother Christian here."—MP 58.

Then too, as he tells in his *Testament* 282, loving care of the lepers sealed his conversion.

139. There was a feeling for people too embarrassed to speak the request in their eyes, as for the woman who asked his blessing one day. A little encouragement and the story of high intent opposed by a contrary husband was out.

"Go, blest daughter, and be assured that soon you will be comforted regarding your husband. But tell him, on God's part and mine, that this is the moment of salvation, and presently there will be the time of fair requital."

And a very holy husband he proved to be.— 2C 38.

140. Hard things too he might do and say to people when a higher good was at stake for them or others:

"Look, brother host, won by your entreaties I have entered your home for a meal. But now, hurry and comply with my directions. You are not to eat here but somewhere else. Confess your sins with all devotion and contrition; let not a thing be left undisclosed in a good confession. Today the Lord is going to pay you back for having welcomed his poor with such great attachment."

It was his way of saying the man was to die
that day, as actually happened.—TRM 41.

141. There was the sick dignitary whose sins
had caught up with him, and who cried for Francis's blessing:

"After you have all this time been living
according to the lusts of the flesh, how am I
to mark you with the sign of the Cross? Still,
because of the devoted prayers of those inter-
ceding for you, I will mark you with the sign
of the Cross in the name of the Lord.

"But mind that if you get relief and return
to your vomit, you are going to suffer worse
affliction. Worse things than the first are
always inflicted for the sin of ingratitude."—
B 11.

142. A little ruse to help the poor? Not that
he sought it, but once when rich persons pressed
the loan of some exquisite garments on shivering
Francis:

"I will accept this from you with the understanding that you do not ever expect it back
again."—1C 76.

Nobody needed to tell draper's son Francis
what those clothes would bring for the poor!

Part VI

Saint Francis
Addresses himself
to his Brothers

PART VI

St. Francis addresses himself
to his brothers

143. Time and again St. Francis called his rule "the book of life, the hope of our salvation, the pledge of our glory, the marrow of the Gospel, the way of the Cross, the state of perfection, the key of Paradise, the contract of our eternal covenant."—MP 76.

144. Again and again he insisted that

"as the Lord has given it to me to speak and write the rule and these words simply and purely, thus simply and purely are you to understand them and with holy practice to observe them to the last."—Cf. Testament **282i.**

145. He used to say, that brother would be *the ideal Lesser Brother* who presented the life and circumstances of these holy brothers:

"The loyalty of Brother Bernard—he had it in a most perfect degree along with his love of holy poverty;

the simplicity and purity of Brother Leo—

a man of truly the most holy purity:

the courtesy of Brother Angelo, the first knight to come into the order, a man graced with all courtesy and gentleness;

the gracious mien and inborn sensitiveness of Brother Masseo, together with his fair, devout language;

the mind of Brother Giles, elevated in contemplation to the utmost perfection;

Brother Rufino's virtuous, continuous gift of prayer, who prayed always, without let-up —even sleeping, or at work otherwise, his mind was always with God;

the patience of Brother Juniper—he arrived at a state of perfect patience by accepting the exact truth as to his own uselessness (which he kept before his eyes continually) and by desiring sovereignly to imitate Christ on the way of the Cross;

the bodily and spiritual prowess of Brother John Lodi—in those days stronger of body than any other men;

the charity of Brother Roger—all his life and manner were a fervor of charity;

the solicitous concern of Brother Lucido— his conscientiousness was of the greatest, and scarcely would he stay in any place a month at a time—the moment he found pleasure staying at a place he promptly left it, saying, 'We have no lasting sojourn here, but in Heaven'."—MP 85.

146. The brothers' watchword was to be*:

"Go, and cast your care upon the Lord, and he will provide for you."—1C 29.

147. The concern and joy of Francis were brothers who were *given to prayer*:

"Those are my knights of the Round Table, who keep hidden in remote, desert places the more earnestly to spend their time in prayer and meditation, deploring their sins and the sins of others, plain of life and humble of manner; whose holiness is known to God, but at times unknown to their brothers and to the people.

"When the souls of these men are presented to the Lord by the angels, the Lord will show them the fruit and wages of their labors in the many souls saved by their example, prayers and tears, and he will say to them, 'My beloved children, look, so and so many souls have been saved through your prayers, tears, and example. Because you have been faithful over a few things I will place you over many things'."—MP 72.

148. He wrote a special statute or instruction for those who would retire to hermitages:

RELIGIOUS LIFE IN A HERMITAGE

"Those who wish to spend the time religiously in hermitages, should be three brothers or at most four together. Let two of them act as the mothers, and have the other two as their children, or at least the one. The two former should lead the life of Martha while the two others lead the life of Mary Magdalene.

"Let those who lead the life of Mary have one cloister, but each his own quarters in it, so that they do not live or sleep in the same quarters. And let them always say the Compline for the day when the sun is about to set, and let them be careful to keep silence and say their Hours and get up for the Matins; and let them seek first the kingdom of God and his justice (Mt. 6, 33). And at the proper time let them say the Prime and the Tierce, and after the hour of the Tierce they may end the silence and can speak and go to their mothers, and, when they wish, they may ask them for an alms for the love of the Lord God, like tiny poor people. And after that let them say the Sext and the None and the Vespers at the required time.

"And they must not let anybody come into the cloister where they live, nor let them eat there. And the brothers who are the mothers should endeavor to keep distant from everybody and in obedience to their custos guard their children from everybody, so that nobody can speak with them. The children themselves should not speak with anybody but to the mothers and their custos, when it pleases him to visit them with God's blessing. The children in turn should now and then take over the duty of the mothers as they will have found it well to arrange the change for a time. And then they shall endeavor to observe carefully and faithfully everything said above."—O 83 to 84.

149. Even on the road, the brothers should make a cell of their body:

"In the name of the Lord go your way two and two, humbly, decorously, and in particular amid strict silence from early morning till after the Tierce, praying in your hearts to the Lord. Idle and useless words are not to be uttered between you.

"For though you walk abroad, let your manner nevertheless be as humble and decorous as if you were in a hermitage or a cell. For wherever we are and go, we have our cell with us. Brother Body is our cell, and our soul is the hermit living indoors in the cell, in order to pray to God and meditate on him. If his soul does not remain in retirement in its cell, any hand-built cell is of little use to a religious."—MP 65.

150. No hard prayers were required:

"When you pray, say the Our Father and, 'We adore you, most holy Lord Jesus Christ, here and at all your churches all over the world, and we bless you; because by your holy Cross you have redeemed the world'."
—1C 45.*

151. Read? Yes, but meditate above all:

"It is good to read what Scripture testifies, good to seek out our Lord in it. For my part, I have fixed in mind so much of the Scriptures that it now suffices most amply for my meditation and reflection. I do not need very much, my son: I know about poor Christ crucified!"—2C 105.

152. And as for *suffering*, temptation and trial:

"Do not be afraid because you are tempted. The more you are beset by temptation, the greater servant and friend of God do I consider you. I tell you that nobody in fact ought to consider himself a perfect friend of God except insofar as he passes through many trials and temptations."—LF 2nd Stigm.

153. "A temptation vanquished is so to say the ring with which the Lord espouses to himself the soul of his servant. Many there are who flatter themselves on merits of years' standing and feel happy at having undergone no temptations. They should know that because the fright of it alone, previous to the clash, would overwhelm them, their weakness of spirit was taken into account by the Lord. Vigorous contests are scarcely put up to people except where their ability has been perfected."—2C 118.

154. Indeed, why not suffer now? Is Purgatory preferable?

"Even a perfect religious often sins without making note of it. In those whom the Lord loves with tender love, he does not allow anything to remain unpunished in this life."
—MP 67.

155. Virtue is preserved at the expense of *severe discipline:*

"Overgreat security leads to lessened caution against the enemy. If the Devil can get hold of a single hair of a man, he soon has it enlarged to a cable. And if for years on end he is not able to down the person he has been tempting, he does not haggle over the delay so long as the person gives in to him in the end. That is his business. He thinks of nothing else day and night."—2C 113.

156. "When the spirit is lukewarm and gradually cooling to grace, flesh and blood needs seek their own. What is left, when the soul finds no delights, but that the flesh turns to its kind? And then animal appetite uses the argument of necessity as a pall. Then the carnal sense shapes a person's conscience.

"Suppose my brother is in real need. Suppose any lack of necessities touches him. If he hastens to satisfy it and drive it far off, what is he to have in reward? He did have an opportunity for merit, but he deliberately proved it was not agreeable to him."

"Exact observance," he added sadly, "will

yet be so far relaxed, tepidity so prevalent, that the sons of their poor father will not blush to wear scarlet silks, just changing the color."—2C 69.

157. Sooner suffer need than make the first concession:

"Suppose on account of need and poverty brother body cannot have what he needs in health and illness, or that it is not given to him when he asks his brother or superior for it humbly and politely for the love of God, then let him suffer it patiently for the love of God, who likewise waited for someone to comfort him and found no one.

"Such need borne with patience will be counted as martyrdom for him by the Lord. And because he did what he should, in humbly asking for what he needed, he is not guilty of sin though his body grow the more seriously ill for it."—MP 97.

158. *Poverty* should be the basic principle. Having, leads to pride and avarice:

"After you get a psalter, you will crave and ask for a breviary. And when you get the breviary, you will sit in state like some prelate and say to your brother, Go fetch me my breviary! . . . Me, a breviary! Me, a breviary!"—MP 4.

159. Be slow to break the rule even on the plea of charity. When asked to reserve some entrants' property to provide for numerous brother guests:

"Away with such fraternal regard that for anybody's sake there would be sinful action against the rule. Strip the altar of the Bl. Virgin and take away its furnishings, if you have no other way to provide for the needy. Believe me, she will be more pleased to have her son's Gospel observed and her altar stripped, than to have her altar in trim and her Son disregarded. The Lord will send someone to restore to his Mother what she has lent us."—2C 67.

160. When a brother companion suggested they pick up a lost purse to give it to the poor:

"Son, it is wrong for us to carry off what belongs to another. It is sin deserving punishment, not merit deserving glory, to make donation of other people's things."

Then, when a serpent crept out of it:

"See there? To God's servants money is nothing but the Devil and a venomous snake." —2C 68.

161. "Let us, who have given up everything, take care lest for anything as cheap as wordly goods we should lose the kingdom of Heaven. If we find money anywhere, let us give it no more thought than the dust under our feet."—LTC 9.

162. Feast days? Oh yes, but in keeping! Not feasting days!

"The lessons of poverty given us by the Son of God ought to motivate us more than other religious. I saw a well laid and decorated table here, and I had to think it was not that of poor people who beg from door to door."

Francis sat down on the floor with a plain dish in his lap:

"Now I am seated like a Lesser Brother!" —2C 61.

163. "On the day of Christ the poor, you want to deviate from holy poverty? Mind that on this day the Bl. Virgin scarcely had bread to eat and the Lord of the world had an animal's crib for his cradle. Imitate your poor father. Keep in mind the wailing of the little Infant."—2 Conformities 4.

164. Nobody to be poorer than he and his:

"This man's state of need shames us greatly, reproaches our poverty very strongly . . . I chose poverty as my wealth, as my lady, and look, it shines more brightly in him. Are you unaware that the report is noised all over the world that for the love of Christ we are the most extremely poor of men? This man is proof that it is otherwise."—2C 84.

165. Begging for deserved alms should be an honor:

"Blest be the brother of mine who goes out promptly, makes the quest humbly, and comes back happy."—2C 76.

166. One brother was "zero at questing but several at table." Francis said to him:

"Go your way, brother fly! You want to eat up the sweat of your brothers and be idle at God's work. You are like brother drone. He does not take on the toil of the bees but wants the first chance eating the honey."

"The nobler a son of mine is, the more readily let him go on the errand. In that way merits are heaped up for him."—2C 75.

167. *Chastity* to him was a matter of not trifling with occasions:

"Why should not anybody fear to gaze at a bride of Christ? Inasfar as eyes and countenance can preach, it is for her to look at me, not me at her."—2C 114.

168. "What matters has a Lesser Brother to transact with a woman except when she has a matter of conscience to propose regarding the holy path of penance and advice toward a better life?"—2C 114.

169. There was his precious Parable of the Two Messengers:

"A powerful king sent two messengers in

succession to his queen. The first one came back and gave a strictly word for word report; for he had the eyes of a wise man in his head and they never popped about. The second one returned, and after the brief words of his report he spun a long story about the lady's beauty: 'Truly, my lord, I have seen a very beautiful woman. Happy the man who enjoys her.' But the king said: 'You good-for-nothing caitiff, have you been casting wanton eyes on my spouse? Plainly you meant to buy the article you examined so minutely.'

"Then he ordered the first messenger to be called back and said to him: 'What do you think of the queen?' Said he: 'Oh, very much: she listened in silence, she answered shrewdly.' Said the king: 'And is there no fairness about her?' 'My lord,' said the man, 'it is for you to look at that; it was my duty to convey the message.'

"The king then passed sentence saying: 'Chaste of eye as you are, in my chamber be still more chaste of body. But let that fellow get out of my house, lest he defile my couch'."
—2C 113.

170. No idleness! Both to prevent mischief and to be no public burden:

"I want my brothers to toil and exert themselves, lest, if they give way to idleness, they stray into forbidden paths with heart or tongue."—B 5. Cf. **282d**.

171. *Obedience* was the final word in true poverty to Francis—the renunciation of the ego:

"My dearest brothers, obey orders at the first utterance. Do not wait for what is said to be repeated. And do not talk about impossibilities, for even if I were to order anything beyond your strength, your obedience would not lack the strength for it."—2C 51.

172. True obedience stands not only by what is said exteriorly but also by what is in the mind:

"If a subject brother not only hears the voice of his brother superior but knows what his wish is, he ought promptly to gather himself for total obedience and do what he understands the superior to be intending."—1C 45.

173. Perfect obedience?

"There is scarcely a religious in all the world that obeys his superior perfectly!

"Take a corpse and put it where you please. You will see, it does not resent being moved, nor grumble at the place it is put, nor want back the place it left. Seat it on high, it will not look up, but down. Surround it with purple, you double its pallor.

"That is your true obedient person. He does not reason about why he is moved, does not mind where he is placed, does not insist on a transfer elsewhere. Raised to office, he keeps his habitual humility. The more he is honored, the more unworthy he regards himself."—2C 152.

174. Francis said actions granted on request were properly speaking permissions, whereas actions enjoined and not requested were true acts of holy obedience. Both were good, but the second safer.—2C 152.

175. The supreme act of obedience, one in which flesh and blood had no share, was the act by which one went by Divine inspiration among unbelievers, be it for the benefit of one's neighbor, or from the desire of martyrdom. He regarded it as very pleasing to God also to ask for this permission.—2C 152.

176. Again and again his words and writings stress fraternal, rather maternal, *charity*. Typical:

"I want my brothers to act like children of the same mother among themselves; and that if one should ask for a tunic or a cord or whatever else, the other should give it freely. Let them share their books and everything that is agreeable, indeed let each force the other to take the things."—2C 180.

177. He was alert for breaches of charity:

"How did your companion act toward you on this journey?"

"Oh, quite all right, Father."

"Brother, be careful lest you be fibbing on pretext of humility. I know how he acted toward you. Just wait awhile and you shall see."

The bullying elder left the order.—2C 39.

178. He abominated backbiting:

"The malice of detraction is greater than that of robbers, inasmuch as the law of Christ, which finds its fulfilment in charity, binds us to desire the welfare of people's soul more than that of their body."—B 8.

179. Example meant everything:

"The best brothers are put to embarrassment by what bad brothers do, and where the good have not sinned, they suffer censure as a result of the example of the wicked." —2C 157.

180. "The time will come when God's beloved order will be so defamed by evil example that it will be ashamed to appear in public. Those, however, who at that time will come to embrace the order, will be led solely by the operation of the Holy Spirit, and flesh and blood will attach no stain to them, and they will be blest truly of the Lord.

"And even if—with the charity that makes saints work with fervor, growing cold—there be no meritorious works in them, there will be measureless trials coming over them, and

those who in that period will be found standing the test, will be better than their prede-
cessors. Woe, however, to those who, flatter-
ing themselves on the mere appearance of
religious living, go numb with apathy and do
not resist steadfastly the trials permitted to
test the elect; because only those who stand
approved will receive the crown of life. But
meantime the guile of the wicked goes on
exercising them."—2C 157.

181. On the other hand, he used to insist that
the largest crowd of imperfect men is outshone
by the virtue of a single saint, for immeasurable
darkness gives way at the beam of a single light.
—2C 158.

182. Above all he wanted to see *good cheer*
from first to last of the brothers. To a young
recruit who, as it proved, had entered from pique:

"You wretched, carnal lad! What makes
you think you can lie to the Holy Ghost and
me? You are weeping for reasons of the flesh,
and your heart is not with God. Go your way,
for you have no spiritual appreciation of
anything."—2C 40.

183. Another case was the brother praised by
the rest—so holy he would not go to confession
lest he break silence. He ended a criminal, "deprived of both Penance and life":

"Stop, brothers, sing me not the praises of
what in his case are the figments of the Devil.

Take it as certain, this is a devilish temptation and fraudulent deceit. Just admonish
him to go to confession once or twice a week;
if he does not go, you will know that what I
am saying is true."—2C 28.

184. "It is for the Devil and his limbs to
be sad, but for us always to be cheerful and
happy in the Lord."—MP 95.

185. "If the servant of God studies to
have and keep, within and without, that
spiritual cheerfulness which proceeds from
a clean heart and is acquired by devotion to
prayer, the evil spirits cannot harm him ...
But the demons are elated when they can
extinguish or in a measure interfere with the
devotion and joy proceeding from prayer that
is pure, and from other virtuous actions."
—MP 95.

186. "The Devil exults most when he can
steal a man's joy of spirit from him. He
carries a powder with him to throw into any
smallest possible chinks of our conscience, to
soil the spotlessness of our mind and the
purity of our life. But when spiritual joy fills
our hearts, the Serpent pours out his deadly
poison in vain.

"The demons cannot hurt a servant of
Christ when they see him filled with holy
mirth. But when his spirit is tearful, forlorn,
downcast, it is readily swallowed up com-

pletely by sadness, or it is carried to the extreme of vain enjoyments . . . When a servant of God, as commonly happens, is troubled about anything, he ought to get right up and pray, and insist on staying in his sovereign Father's presence until He restores the joy of his salvation to him. For if he lingers in his gloom, that Babylonian mess will ripen to the point where, if it is not flushed out with tears, it will generate permanent corrosion in the heart."—2C 125.

187. "Why do you show your sorrow and sadness for your sins exteriorly? Keep such sadness between yourself and God, and pray that in his mercy he may pardon you and give back to your soul the gladness of his salvation of which it has been deprived by the demerit of sin. But before me and the rest try always to have a cheerful air; it does not become a servant of God to appear before his brother or anybody else with sadness and a troubled countenance."—MP 96.

188. "Settle accounts with your failings in your room; there weep and sigh in God's presence. When you come back among your brothers, put gloom aside and be like the rest . . .

"The envious rivals of man's salvation bear a big grudge against me: they keep trying to disturb in my companions the man they cannot disturb in me."—2C 128.

189. Always, not only in physical but also in spiritual distress, the brothers had the consolation of St. Francis:

"God is mighty enough, should it please his sweet will, to drive off the cloud of darkness and extend over us the blessing of light."—B 5.

190. Things change, and the brothers must be ready for the sifting process:

"Brothers, that we may faithfully and devotedly give thanks to the Lord our God for all his gifts, and that you may know what life will be like among the brothers present and future, understand what is really going to happen. Now at the beginning of our way of life we are going to find certain fruits exceedingly sweet and pleasant to eat, but a little later certain less sweet and pleasant fruits will be offered; then at length certain fruits will be given us that are full of bitterness and that we cannot eat; because of their bitterness nobody will be able to stomach them although they may have some outward show of fragrance and fairness.

"Now, as I have told you, the Lord will really increase us to be a great people. But finally it will happen just as when a man casts his nets into the sea or into some lake: he hauls in a copious multitude of fish, but when he has put them all in his boat, not caring to take them all along on account of their number, he singles out the larger and more suitable ones for his baskets but throws the rest out."—1C 28.

191. It is in his larger writings that St. Francis shows his loving interest in the brothers to best advantage. He displays deep knowledge of human nature as well as practical sense.

There are his *Admonitiones* or Reminders to the brothers, so much of a piece that it would be a pity to separate them (O 1-19):

THE REMINDERS OF ST. FRANCIS

1. *The Blessed Sacrament*

Our Lord Jesus said to his disciples: "I am the way, the truth, and the life. Nobody can come to the Father except through me. If you had recognized me, you would have recognized my Father too. And from now on you will recognize him, since you have seen him." Philip said to him: "Lord, show us the Father and it is enough for us." Jesus said to him: "Have I been so long a time with you and you have not learned who I am? Philip, whoever sees me, sees my Father too" (Jn. 14, 6-9).

Now, the Father dwells in light that cannot be penetrated (1 Tim. 6, 16), and God is a spirit (Jn. 4, 24), and nobody has ever seen

God (Jn. 1, 18). Because God is a spirit, therefore he can be seen only by means of the spirit; for it is the spirit that gives life, whereas the flesh is of no avail (Jn. 6, 64).

But since the Son is like the Father, he too is seen by nobody otherwise than the Father is seen, or otherwise than the Holy Spirit is seen. And so it was that those who saw our Lord Jesus Christ only in a human way and did not see nor believe that he was the true Son of God, as the spirit and his Divine nature demand—they all stood condemned.

And so now with all those who see the Blessed Sacrament, sanctified by our Lord's words on the altar, through the hands of the priest, in the form of bread and wine: if they do not see and believe, as the spirit and the Divine nature demand, that it is truly the most holy Body and Blood of our Lord Jesus Christ, they stand condemned. For it is the Most High who bears witness to it. He says, "This is my body, and the blood of the New Testament" (Mk. 14, 22-24), and, "He who eats my flesh and drinks my blood, has life everlasting" (Jn. 6, 55).

Thus it is the spirit of the Lord, which dwells in those who believe in him, that truly receives the most holy Body and Blood of our Lord. All the rest, who have nothing of that spirit and presume to receive him, eat and drink judgment to themselves (1 Cor. 11, 29).

So, you children of men, how long is your sense going to stay dull (Ps. 4, 3)? Why do you not see into the truth and believe in the Son of God (Jn. 9, 35)? See, day after day he humbles himself, as when he came down from his royal throne (Wis. 18, 15) into the Virgin's womb. Day by day he comes to us personally in this lowly form. Daily he comes down from the bosom of his Father on the altar into the hands of the priest.

And just as he appeared before the holy Apostles in true flesh, so now he has us see him in the sacred bread. Looking at him with the eyes of their flesh, they saw only his flesh, but regarding him with the eyes of the spirit, they believed that he was God. In like manner, as we see bread and wine with our bodily eyes, let us see and believe firmly that it is his most holy Body and Blood, true and living.

For in this way our Lord is ever present among those who believe in him, according to what he said: "Behold, I am with you all days even to the consummation of the world" (Mt. 28, 20).

2. *The evil of self-will*

191a. The Lord said to Adam: "Eat of any tree in the garden, but of the tree of knowledge of good and evil do not eat" (Gen. 2, 16).

So, Adam could eat the fruit of any tree in Paradise, and he committed no sin so long as he did not act against obedience.

A person eats the fruit of the knowledge of good when he takes his will as his own and prides himself on whatever good the Lord utters and does in him. In that way, on the suggestion of the Devil and transgression of a commandment, it proves to be fruit of the knowledge of evil to him, and so it is as it should be if he suffers the penalty for it.

3. *Perfect and imperfect obedience*

191b. Our Lord says in the Gospel: "Whoever does not renounce everything he possesses, cannot be my disciple" (Lk. 14, 33), and, "Whoever seeks to save his life, will lose it" (Mt. 16, 25).

That person gives up everything he possesses and loses body and life, who keeps himself altogether ready for obedience at the hands of his superior; and whatever he does or says is true obedience so long as he knows it is not against his superior's will, provided of course that what he does is good.

And if ever a subject finds anything better and more useful for his soul than what his superior orders, let him nevertheless sacrifice his will to God and set himself to suit his actions to his superior's wishes. For obedience is true and in keeping with holy charity when it satisfies both God and neighbor.

Should a superior, however, give a subject an order that is contrary to his conscience, then, though he do not obey him, the subject should not disown him; and should he have to suffer persecution from this or that superior for it, let him love them the more for the love of God. For a person that would sooner suffer persecution than be parted from his brethren, certainly abides in perfect obedience, since he is staking his life for his brethren (cf. Jn. 15, 13).

For there are many religious who on the pretext of seeing something better than what their superiors order, look backward (cf. Lk. 9, 62) and return to the vomit of their self-will (cf. Prov. 26, 11). Such people are killers and cause many souls to be lost through their bad example.

4. *Nobody should grasp at superiorship*

191c. "I have not come to be ministered to, but to minister," says our Lord (Mt. 20, 28).

Those who are placed above others, should pride themselves on their preferment no more than if they had been appointed to the charge of washing the feet of their brethren; and if they are disturbed any more about having their preferment taken from them

than the charge of washing feet, they are by
so much piling up accounts to the peril of
their soul.

5. *Nobody should be proud, but find glory in the Cross of our Lord*

191d. Observe, O man, to what distinction the Lord has raised you in creating you
and molding you according to the image of
his beloved Son bodily and according to his
likeness spiritually (cf. Gen. 1, 26).

Yet all the creatures under heaven in their
way serve, recognize and obey their Creator
better than you do. And even the demons
did not crucify him, but you with their help
crucified him and still crucify him when you
take pleasure in vice and sin.

So, on what grounds can you glory?

For if you were as subtle and wise as to
possess all knowledge and explain any kind
of language and penetrate keenly into the
mysteries of Heaven, you could not glory in
any of it, since any demon once knew more
about heavenly matters and now knows more
about earthly matters than all mortals,
though there might be a person who had
received of the Lord a special insight into the
sovereign Wisdom.

In like manner if you were more handsome
or wealthy than anybody, and even if you
could perform marvels enough to put the

demons to flight, all such things are on your debit side and in no way belong to you, and you have no right whatever to take pride in them.

But what we can take credit for are our infirmities (cf. 2 Cor. 12, 5), and that day by day we have the holy cross of our Lord Jesus Christ to carry.

6. *Imitating our Lord*

191e. As brothers all, let us observe the Good Shepherd, who to save his sheep underwent the suffering of the Cross.

The Lord's sheep have taken after him in hardship and persecution and disgrace, in hunger and thirst, in infirmity and trial and other such things (cf. Jn. 10, 11; Jn. 10, 4; Hebr. 12, 2; Rom. 8, 35), and for that they received life everlasting from the Lord.

So it is a great shame for us servants of God, that the saints did the work and we want to get the honor and glory for it by talking and preaching about it.

7. *Good works should follow on knowledge*

191f. The Apostle says, "The letter kills, but the spirit gives life" (2 Cor. 3, 6).

They are slain by the letter who only crave to know the words of it, so that they can pass as more learned than others and acquire great riches to leave to their relatives and friends.

And those religious are slain by the letter

who have no will to follow the spirit of God's written word, but rather desire to know only the text and explain it to others.

And those people draw life from the spirit of God's written word who do not lay out on personal advantage whatever they know or seek to know of the Divine Scriptures, but by word and example give it back to the sovereign Lord, to whom all good things belong.

8. *Avoiding the sin of envy*

191g. The Apostle says, "Nobody can say, Jesus is the Lord, except in the Holy Spirit" (1 Cor. 12, 3), and it says, "There is no one that does anything good, no, not one" (Ps. 52, 4).

So it is that whoever envies his brother for the good which the Lord says or does in him, comes close to the sin of blasphemy, because his envy touches the Most High, since it is he who says and does whatever is good.

9. *Charity*

191h. Our Lord says in the Gospel: "Love your enemies," and so forth (Mt. 5, 44).

That person truly loves his enemy who does not grieve over the injury done to himself, but for the love of God is on fire over the sin on the person's soul and proceeds to show his love for him by his actions.

10. *Chastising the body*

191i. There are many who, when they commit sin or suffer any wrong, often blame their enemy or their neighbor.

But that is not so, because everybody has his real enemy in his own power, and that enemy is his own person when he sins with it.

So, blessed is the servant who always keeps that enemy thus given into this power, under control and guards himself prudently against him; for, let him do that, and no enemy visible or invisible can do him any harm.

11. *Nobody to worsen at another's fault*

191j. Nothing ought to be disagreeable to a servant of God but sin. And no matter how anybody else may sin, if a servant of God gets disturbed or angry over it except out of charity, he heaps up guilt for himself (cf. Rom. 2, 5).

The servant of God that does not get angry or upset on anyone's account, lives as is right, and without sin.

And blessed is the person who does not keep anything back for himself, giving Caesar what is Caesar's and God what is God's (Mt. 22, 21).

12. *Recognizing the spirit of the Lord*

191k. You can tell by this whether a servant of God has anything of the spirit of God, that, when the Lord does anything good

through him, his flesh, in its constant opposition to everything good, is not puffed up
about it and he rather regards himself the
more unworthy in his own eyes and considers
himself inferior to all other people.

13. *Patience*

1911. You cannot tell what degree of patience and humility a servant of God has
about him as long as he has been having his
way.

But let the time come when those who
should oblige him, do the contrary to him,
and what degree of patience and humility he
has then, that is the degree he has and no
more.

14. *Poverty of spirit*

191m. "Blessed are the poor in spirit, for
theirs is the kingdom of Heaven" (Mt. 5, 3).

There are many people that devote themselves to prayers and devotions, and practice
bodily restrictions and afflictions of many
kinds, but at a single word that seems offen-
sive to their person, or at anything taken
away from them, they are quickly scandalized
and upset.

Such people are not poor in spirit, because
anyone that is truly poor in spirit, hates
himself and loves those who slap him in
the face (cf. Mt. 5, 39).

15. *Peacemakers*

191n. "Blessed are the peacemakers, for they shall be called children of God" (Mt. 5, 9).

They are truly friends of peace who, no matter what they have to suffer in the world, still preserve peace within and without for love of our Lord Jesus Christ.

16. *The clean of heart*

191o. "Blessed are the pure of heart, for they shall see God" (Mt. 5, 8).

They are pure of heart who disregard what the world offers and seek what Heaven offers, never ceasing to adore and contemplate the true and living Lord God with a clean heart and mind.

17. *The humble servant of God*

191p. Blessed is the servant that is no more elated at the good which the Lord says and does through him than at that which He says and does through anybody else.

It is sinful of a person to be more set on receiving from his neighbor than he is willing to give of himself to the Lord God.

18. *Sympathy with one's neighbor*

191q. Blessed is the person that puts up with the frailty of his neighbor to the extent he would like his neighbor to put up with him if he were in a similar plight.

19. *The blessed and the blameworthy servant*

191r. Blessed is the servant that returns all the goods he has to the Lord God.

For whoever withholds anything for himself, hides away his Lord's money on his own person (Mt. 25, 18), and so, what he thinks he has, will be taken from him (Lk. 8, 18).

20. *The good and humble religious*

191s. Blessed is the servant that does not think himself any the better when people make much of him and exalt him than when they consider him worthless, ordinary, and contemptible. For what a person is before God, so much he is, and no more.

Woe to that religious that is elevated by his fellow religious and is of no mind to get down from his rank of his own accord. And blessed is the servant who is elevated through no will of his own and is always minded to keep at the feet of the rest.

21. *The blessed and the useless religious*

191t. Blessed is that religious that takes no pleasure and delight except in the very holy things our Lord said and did, and uses them to lead people to cheerful and happy love of God.

And woe to that religious that finds his delight in idle and frivolous talk and makes use of it to make people laugh.

22. *The empty and talkative religious*

191u. Blessed is the servant that does not speak in the hope of gain, and does not tell everything about himself, and is not hasty to speak (Prov. 29, 20) but prudently weighs beforehand the proper thing to say and reply.

Woe to that religious that does not keep safe in his heart the treasures the Lord has shown him and, instead of revealing them to others by his conduct, seeks to disclose them to people in his conversation for the sake of a requital. Such a person gets his reward in that way, and his listeners have little fruit to show for it.

23. *Genuine correction*

191v. Blessed is the servant that takes direction, blame, and reproof as patiently from anyone else as from himself.

Blessed is the servant that on being reproved cheerfully agrees, modestly complies, humbly confesses, and readily makes amends.

Blessed is the servant that is not quick to excuse himself, and humbly accepts the embarrassment and the reproof for a sin where he was not guilty of any fault.

24. *Genuine humility*

191w. Blessed is the person that is found to be as humble among his dependents as if he were among his superiors.

Blessed is the servant that always keeps under the rod of correction.

The faithful and prudent servant (Mt. 24, 45) is he that, whatever his offenses, is not slow to punish them interiorly by contrition and exteriorly by confession and works of atonement.

25. *Genuine charity*

191x. Blessed is the brother that would love his brother in illness, when the brother cannot be of use to him, as much as he loves him in health, when he can be of use to him.

Blessed is the brother that would love and respect his brother if he were far away as much as if he were with him, and would say nothing about him behind his back that in all charity he could not say in his presence.

26. *Servants of God honor the clergy*

191y. Blessed the servant of God that remains loyal to the clergy who live duly according to the established order of the Holy Roman Church.

And woe to those who despise them! For, though they be sinners, yet nobody has a right to sit in judgment on them, since the Lord reserves to himself alone the right to judge them.

For just as the ministry they have surpasses all others, concerned as it is with the most holy Body and Blood of our Lord Jesus

Christ, which they receive and they alone administer to others: so do those who sin against them have a greater sin than by sinning against any other people in this world.

27. *The virtues that rout vice*

191z. Where there is charity and wisdom,
there is neither fear nor ignorance.
Where there is patience and humility
there is neither anger nor loss of composure.
Where there is poverty borne with joy,
there is neither grasping nor hoarding.
Where there is quiet and meditation,
there is neither worry nor dissipation.
Where there is the fear of the Lord to guard
the gateway,
there the Enemy can get no hold for an
entry.
Where there is mercy and discernment,
there is neither luxury nor a hardened
heart.

191z1. Blessed is the servant that treasures up for Heaven (Mt. 6, 20) the favors God extends to him, and that has no desire to disclose them to people in the hope of requital, because the Most High himself will make his works known to whomever he wishes.

Blessed the servant that keeps the secrets of the Lord carefully in his heart.

192. And there is the beautiful letter (O 99-107) written "toward the end of his days" to the Chapter General and all the Friars, replete with some of the most stirring passages in literature on reverence toward the Blessed Sacrament and everything related to it.

LETTER TO THE CHAPTER GENERAL AND ALL THE FRIARS

In the name of the sovereign Trinity and the holy Unity Father, Son, and Holy Ghost.

To the brethren all, so worthy of reverence and great love; to his master the Minister General of the Order of Friars Minor, and the other ministers general to come after him; to the ministers and custodes and priests of the same brotherhood all, so humble in Christ; and to all the plain and obedient brothers, first and last:

Brother Francis, a paltry, feeble man, your poor little servant, gives greeting in Him who has redeemed and washed us in his precious Blood; on hearing whose name you should adore him prostrate on the ground in awe and reverence, for the Lord Jesus Christ, the Son of the Most High, is his name, and he is blest forever. Amen.

192a. Listen, children of the Lord and my brothers, and with your ears take up my words. Turn the ear of your heart to the voice of the Son of God and obey it. With all your heart keep his commandments, and fulfil his counsels with a perfect will. Proclaim it that he is good, and in what you do, glorify him (Tob. 6, 8), because he has sent you all over the world so that you should bear witness to his voice in word and deed, and have everybody learn that there is no one almighty but he. Persevere under holy discipline and obedience, and with a good and firm resolution comply with what you have promised him. For God our Lord deals with you as with his children (Heb. 12, 7).

192b. So, I entreat you all, brothers, with a kiss for your feet and whatever charity I can, to bring all the reverence and all the respect you ever can to bear on the most holy Body and Blood of our Lord Jesus Christ, through whom whatever there is in Heaven and on earth has been appeased and reconciled (Col. 1, 20) to God almighty.

I likewise beg in the Lord all my brothers who now are and will be and wish to be priests of the Most High that when they wish to celebrate Mass, they should be pure and in a pure and reverent manner perform the true sacrifice of the most holy Body and Blood of our Lord Jesus Christ with a clean and holy intention, and not for any earthly return or out of fear or love of any man, as if to please men. But let all their will, so far as the grace of the Almighty favors, be directed

toward him, in the desire to please with it the
sovereign Lord alone, because in it he alone
acts, as it pleases him. For, now that he says,
"Do this for a commemoration of me," if
anybody acts otherwise, he becomes Judas
the traitor, and makes himself guilty of the
body and blood of our Lord.

192c. Remember, my priest brothers, what
is written about the law of Moses: those
transgressing it, though it were in material
ways, died without any mercy, according to
the Lord's decree (Heb. 10, 28). How much
greater and worse penalties does he deserve
to suffer who has trodden the Son of God un-
derfoot, who has treated as unclean the blood
of the Testament through which he has been
sanctified, and has offered an insult to the
Spirit of grace? (Heb. 10, 29.)

For a person despises, soils and tramples on
the Lamb of God when, as the Apostle says,
he does not make a difference and distinguish
between the holy Bread of Christ and other
foods and actions, or when he eats it while
unworthy or, if worthy, then in an idle and
improper manner, since the Lord says in the
words of the Prophet, "Cursed the man who
does the work of the Lord deceitfully" (Jer.
48, 10). And spurning those priests who do
not bother to take this to heart, he will say:
"I will curse your blessings" (Mal. 2, 2).

192d. Listen, my brothers: If the Blessed
Virgin Mary is honored so much—and rightly
so—because she bore him about in her most
holy womb; if the blessed Baptist trembled
all over and did not dare to touch the holy
crown of his God; if the tomb in which he lay
for a while is venerated so much: then how
holy, just and worthy ought the person to be
who freely handles him, receives him in
mouth and heart, and presents him for others
to receive, not in a mortal state any more, but
as going to live and as glorified forever,
"whom the angels yearn to gaze upon" (1
Pet. 1, 12).

192e. Look at your dignity, priestly
brothers, and be holy because he is holy. And
as the Lord God has honored you more than
all people by means of this mystery, so should
you love, revere and honor him more than all
people. It is a great pity and a pitiable weakness that you should have him thus present
and still be interested in anything else in all
the world.

Let everything in man halt in awe, let all
the world quake, and let Heaven exult when
Christ, the Son of the living God, is there on
the altar in the hands of the priest! Oh, ad-
mirable dignity and amazing condescension!
Oh, sublime lowliness! Oh, lowly sublimity!
That the Lord of the universe, God and the
Son of God, should so humble himself as to

hide under the tiny little form of bread for our welfare. Look, brothers, at the humility of God and pour your hearts out before him. Be humbled yourselves, so you can be exalted by him.

So, do not keep anything about you back for yourselves, so that he may have you altogether as his own who puts himself altogether at your disposal.

192f. So I admonish and exhort you in the Lord, that in the places where the brothers stay, a single Mass in the day be celebrated according to the form of holy Church.* If, however, there are several priests at the place, let each for the love of charity be glad to have heard the celebration of the other, for the present and the absent that are worthy of it, get their fill from the Lord Jesus Christ. And although he is seen to be in several places, he nevertheless remains indivisible and suffers no impairment, but, entire everywhere, he acts as it pleases him, with the Lord God the Father and the Holy Spirit Paraclete, world without end. Amen.

192g. And since whoever is of God hears the words of God, we who are more particularly set aside for the Divine services, ought therefore not only to hear and do what God says: but also, the better to impress on us the majesty of our Creator and our subjection to him, we ought to take care of the vessels and other liturgical articles which contain his holy words. So I admonish all my brothers and encourage them in Christ, that wherever they find any of the written words of God, they should give them all the reverence they can, and if the words are not well put away or lie strewn about improperly anywhere, they should gather them up and put them away so far as they may do so, honoring in the words the Lord who has spoken. For many a thing is sanctified by the words of God (cf. 1 Tim. 4, 5), and it is in virtue of the words of God that the Sacrament of the Altar is brought about.

192h. Furthermore, I confess all my sins, to God the Father and the Son and the Holy Ghost, to the Blessed Mary ever virgin, to all the saints in Heaven and on earth, to the Minister General of this our order as to my venerable lord, to all the priests of our order and to all the rest of my blest brothers. In many ways I have offended through my grievous fault, in particular because I have not kept the rule I have promised the Lord, and I have not said the Office as the rule commands, either from negligence, or due to my infirmity, or because I am an ignorant and simple person.

Therefore, with everything I can I beseech my lord the Minister General that he have the

rule observed without fail by everybody, and
that the clerics may say the Office devoutly
with God in view, not interested in melody of
voice but in harmony of mind, so that voice
may be attuned to mind but mind to God; so
that they may please God with the purity of
their intention rather than gratify the ears of
the people with the blandishment of their
voice.

192i. For this is what I promise firmly to
observe as the Lord gives me the grace, and
this is what I will leave for the brothers who
are with me to observe, in the Office and in
the other established regulations. If any of
the brothers refuse to observe these particulars, I do not regard them as Catholics or as
my brothers, and I do not want to see or
speak with them until they repent of it. I say
the same concerning all those others who go
roving about, to the disregard of regular discipline, since our Lord Jesus Christ gave up
his life sooner than fail of obedience to his
most holy Father.

192j. I, Brother Francis, a useless man
and an unworthy creature of the Lord God,
by our Lord Jesus Christ say to Brother
Elias, the minister of our entire order, and to
all the ministers general who will come after
him, and to the rest of the custodes and
guardians of the brothers who are and shall

be, that they should keep this writing at hand, act according to it, and preserve it carefully. I implore them to watch with care over what is written in it and have it observed faithfully under the pleasure of almighty God now and forever as long as this world lasts.

Blest shall you be by the Lord if you act thus, and the Lord be with you for all eternity. Amen.

192k. Almighty, eternal, just, and merciful God, have us poor wretches for your sake do what we know you want, and have us always want whatever is pleasing to you; so that cleansed interiorly, and interiorly enlightened and aglow with the fire of the Holy Ghost, we may be able to follow the footsteps of your Son, our Lord Jesus Christ. Aided by your sole-saving grace, may we be able to get to you, who in perfect Trinity and simple Unity live and reign and triumph as God almighty world without end. Amen.

Part VII

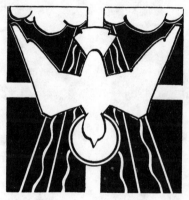

Saint Francis
Addresses himself
to the
Dignitaries

PART VII

St. Francis addresses himself to the dignitaries of the order

193. With his deep sense of responsibility where others were concerned, and his deep consciousness of his own inadequacy, no marvel that St. Francis set high his

IDEAL OF A MINISTER GENERAL

"My son, I see nobody competent to be the leader of an army so manifold and the shepherd of a flock so vast. But I will paint and hand-fashion for you, as the saying is, a man in whom the qualities shine forth which the father of this family ought to have:

"The man ought to be of the utmost moral gravity, of great discernment, of commendable reputation. A man without private affections, lest in favoring any part too much, he engender scandal for the whole. A man fond of the pursuit of prayer, who allots his time between definite hours for his soul and definite hours for the flock committed to him. For he ought to begin early in the morning with the sacred mysteries of the Mass and in extended devotion commend himself and his flock to the protection of God.

"After his prayers he should appear in public at everybody's beck, to respond to everybody, to provide kindly for everybody. He should be a man who will not cut any sordid corner by playing favorites, and who is swayed by no less concern for the lower ranking and witless than for those higher up and gifted. A man who, though it has been granted him to excel by his gift of learning, nonetheless by his conduct rather presents the image of pious simplicity and fosters virtue. A man who execrates money, the chief factor in corrupting the vows and perfection we profess; and who, offering himself as the head of a poor order for the rest to imitate, never is guilty of abuse by having any money. It should be enough for him to have for himself a habit and a notebook, for the brothers' service, however, a pencase and a seal. He should not be a book collector, nor much given to reading, lest he subtract from his duty what he uses up in study.

"A man to console the afflicted, since he is the last refuge of those in trouble, lest, if he be without the healing remedies, the disease of despair prevail against the weak. To incline the high-spirited to meekness, let him abase himself and relent a little of his right, to win a soul for Christ. Let him not close the bowels of his pity toward those who have deserted the order, like the lost sheep they are, knowing that temptations which can drive a person to such a plight, must be overpowering.

"I would wish to have everybody honor him in the stead of Christ and wait on him in whatever is necessary, with all goodwill. It would, however, behoove him not to await honors, nor to take more pleasure in favors than in affronts. If ever, due to weakness or fatigue, he needed more palatable food, he would take it not in private but in public places, to relieve other invalids of their embarrassment in providing for their body. It is his most imperative duty to distinguish hidden motives and to dig the truth out of its secret lodes, not lending an ear to gossips.

"In fine, he ought to be a man who will under no condition endanger the virile framework of justice by his craving to keep the honor, but who will feel that so great an office is bound to be more of a burden than an honor to him. But of course overmuch gentleness must not give rise to indifference, nor lax indulgence to the dissolution of discipline, so that he will be dreaded as much by those who do evil as he is loved by everybody else.

"I would wish, however, that he had associates endowed with a sense of propriety,

who like him would set an example of everything good: men set against self-indulgence,
strong against difficulties, yet so duly affable
that they received anybody coming to them,
with holy geniality.

"See, that is the kind of person the minister
of the order ought to be."—2C 186.

194. Let superiorship be weighed with the eyes
of God:

"It is good and acceptable before God to
have charge of others. Those ought to have
the care of souls who expect nothing for
themselves of it, but heed only the will of
God in all things; men who put nothing above
their salvation; who have regard not for the
applause of their subjects but for their benefit; who care not for show in the sight of men
but for glory before God; who do not aspire
to office but fear it; whom an office conferred
does not make proud but humble, and an
office taken away does not cast down but
lift up."

But at this time especially, when wickedness
has grown so excessive and iniquity has abounded,
he declared, it is perilous to rule and more profit-
able to be ruled.—1C 104.

195. A superior must learn "to take it":

"I do not take myself for a Lesser Brother
unless I shall be of the disposition I will de-
scribe to you:

"Suppose that as the superior of the

brothers I go to the chapter, preach to the brothers, remonstrate with them, and at last they speak up against me: We have no use for an unlettered, inferior man, so we do not want you ruling over us, without all art of expression and plain and unpolished as you are.

"Finally, I am thrown out in disgrace, despised by them all.

"I tell you, unless I listen to that talk with the same brow, the same cheer of mind, and the same determination of holiness, I am by no means a Lesser Brother."—2C 145.

196. It was his opinion that one should rarely command under obedience, shooting the dart at the first which ought to be shot last. . . . But anybody that was unhurried about obeying the order of obedience, had neither fear of God nor respect for man.

"One should not quickly lay hand on sword."—2C 153.

197. Eminence is a pitfall:

"High position occasions downfall; praise, a headlong drop; a subject's humble estate, gain for the soul. Then why are we bent on the danger more than on the gain, after we have once seized on the chance to make such gain?"—2C 145.

198. But it can edify:

"The brothers who are subject are greatly

edified if their ministers and the preachers gladly give their time to prayer and stoop to humble tasks and to services of mean account. Otherwise they cannot without suffering embarrassment, prejudice and censure admonish the rest of the brothers in the matter. They should take the example of Christ and perform before they teach, yes perform and teach at the same time."—MP 73.

199. Severe he could be, as with the minister who wanted to keep certain costly books:

"I do not mean, for the sake of your books, to lose the book of the Gospel which I have pledged. Do just as you please, but you shall not have my permission to serve as a snare." —2C 22.

200. He was especially severe when it came to warning the ministers against whisperers:

"Disruption threatens the order unless the detractors are counteracted. The sweetest odor spread by the many will soon turn to stench unless the stinkers' mouths are gagged. Go to work, investigate carefully, and if you find any accused brother innocent, make his accuser a marked man before everybody, with a severe correction. Push him into the clutches of our Florence pugilist" (Brother John Lodi) "if you cannot punish him yourself. I want you and all the ministers to use the utmost foresight to see that this pestiferous disease spreads no farther."—2C 182.

201. He knew the whisperer's ways:

"This is how the detractor talks: 'I possess no moral perfection, I have no learning or special talent to fall back on, and so I have no standing with God or with men. I know what I will do: I will smear the elect and curry favor with those higher up. I know that my superior is human and that he now and then makes use of the same shift as I to fell the cedars and appear the only shrub in the woods.' Ah, you wretch, go, live on human flesh, and with nothing else to live on, go, gnaw at the vitals of your brothers!"— 2C 183.

202. He revered the preachers, but they had to be men of prayer:

"A preacher ought first in secret prayer to draw the water he intends later to pour out in sacred sermon; he ought to grow warm within before he utters cold words without."

He called it an office to be regarded with reverence, and those who discharged it worthy of veneration by anybody:

"They are the life of the body, the campaigners against the demons, the light of the world."—2C 163.

203. He had little patience with vainglorious preachers:

"Why do you boast about the people you

convert, when my plain brothers have converted them with their prayers?"

He explained the passage, "Until the barren woman has brought forth a great many," by saying:

"The barren woman is my poor little brother, who does not have the office of generating children in the Church. In the Judgment he will bring forth a great many, because the Judge will then set down to his glory the people he is now converting with his private prayers. And the one who has many children will fail, because the preacher who is elated at the many begotten seemingly by his power, will then realize he had no share in them."

He said those divided up a subject badly who bestowed everything on their preaching and nothing on their devotion.—2C 164.

204. Some few writings of St. Francis to his superiors have come down to us. There are three letters "to a Minister," but only one is accounted genuine; the other two are of much the same contents, with lame additions. The minister is commonly taken to be Brother Elias. The letter recommends mercy to the failing, even where the minister himself is failed against:

LETTER TO A CERTAIN MINISTER

"To Brother N., Minister, The Lord bless you:

"I am telling you the best I can in the

matter of your soul, that whatever gives you
trouble in loving the Lord God, and whoever
causes you such trouble, whether it be the
brothers or other people, even were they to
give you a beating, you ought to regard that
as a favor. You should want it that way and
not otherwise. Regard that as true obedience
to the Lord God and to me, for I know posi-
tively that that is true obedience. And love
those who do such things to you, and do not
wish for anything else from them except
whatever the Lord thus gives you, and love
them so far as to wish they might be better
Christians. And let that be of more value to
you than a hermit's life.

"And I will take this as proof of whether
you love the Lord and me, his servant and
yours, if you act as follows: namely, that
there be no brother in the world who has
sinned as much as ever he could sin, yet
who, after looking in your eyes, would ever
go away without mercy from you if he seeks
mercy, and if he were not to seek mercy you
would ask him if he wished for mercy. And if
he appeared before your eyes after that a
thousand times, love him more than me, to
the end that you may drag him to the Lord,
and may you ever have pity on such persons.
And make it known to your guardians when
you can, that you personally are firmly
resolved to act thus.

"As for the several chapters in the rule which speak of mortal sins, with the Lord's help we will at the Pentecost chapter with the advice of the brothers set up a chapter such as this: If anyone of the brothers at the instigation of the Enemy should sin mortally, let him be bound in obedience to have recourse to his guardian. And all the brothers who might know he has sinned, should not cause him embarrassment or loss of honor, but have great pity for him and keep the sin of their brother very secret; for it is not the healthy that need the physician but the ailing (Mt. 9, 12). Likewise let them be bound in obedience to send him with a companion to his custos. The custos should in turn make merciful provision for him as he would wish it made for himself if he were in a similar plight.

"And if he should fall into some venial sin, let him confess it to a priest brother of his, and if there is no priest there, let him confess it to any brother of his, until he shall have a priest to absolve him canonically, as has been said; but the latter shall have no power at all to impose any other penance than this: Go and sin no more.

"To assure the better observance due to it, keep this writing about you till Pentecost; you will be there with your brothers. And these and all other points which are less clearly stated in the rule, you shall with the help of the Lord God take measures to carry out."—O 108-110.

205. The favorite subject of Francis's writings was the Blessed Sacrament. Again and again he comes back to it, as in the

LETTER TO ALL THE CUSTODES

"To all the Custodes of the Lesser Brothers whom this letter will reach, Brother Francis, your servant and little one in the Lord God, welfare, amid the new signs in heaven and on earth, which with the Lord are great and most exceptional but are regarded very lightly by many religious and other people:

"I beseech you more than if it concerned myself, that where it is proper and you find it helpful you may plead humbly with clerics that they ought to venerate above all else the most holy Body and Blood of our Lord Jesus Christ, and writings with his holy names and words, which sanctify the Body. The chalices, corporals, the ornaments of the altar and everything pertaining to the sacrifice, they ought to regard as precious. And if there is any place where the most holy Body of our Lord is lodged very poorly, let it according to the command of the Church be placed by them in a choice place and reserved there, and let it be borne about with great reverence and administered to others with discretion. Also the written names and words of our Lord, wherever found in sordid places, should be picked up and they ought to be put in a decent place.

"And in any preaching you do, admonish the people concerning repentance, and that nobody can be saved except he who receives the most holy Body and Blood of our Lord. And when it is sacrificed on the altar by the priest or borne about anywhere, let all the people on bended knees render praise, glory and honor to the true and living Lord God.

"And tell and preach this to all peoples in his praise, that at every hour and when the bells are rung, praise and thanksgiving should be offered to almighty God by all the people all over the earth.

"And wherever this writing reaches any of my Brother Custodes whatever, and they copy it and keep it about them and cause it to be copied for the brothers who have the office of preaching and the wardenship of the brothers, and preach to the last whatever is contained in this writing: let them know they have the blessing of the Lord God and my own. And let them regard this as true and holy obedience. Amen."—O 113-115.

206. A reminder of the same subject occurs in a questioned letter, one evidently confounded with the above, the

LETTER TO ALL GUARDIANS

"To all the Custodes of the Lesser Brothers whom this letter may reach, Brother Francis, the least of God's servants, wishes welfare and holy peace in the Lord:

"Know that in the sight of God there are certain very high and sublime matters which at times are regarded among men as base and abject; and others are dear and estimable among men which before God are held most base and abject.

"I beseech you before the Lord our God as much as I can that you give the letter dealing with the most holy Body and Blood of our Lord to the bishops and other clergy and that you keep in mind what we have commended to you in it.

"Of the other letter I am sending you, to be given to the rulers, consuls, and governors, wherein it says that God's praises are to be published among the people and throughout the streets, make many copies and samples immediately and give them out to those to whom they are meant to be given.

"Farewell in the Lord."—Opera Omnia S.P.N.F., Wadding-de la Haye, p. 54.

Part VIII

Pax

Saint Francis
Addresses himself
to the Public

PART VIII

St. Francis addresses himself to the public

207. The message of St. Francis to the world was a message of peace:

"The Lord revealed to me that we should speak this greeting: The Lord give you peace."—Testament **282e.**

208. Significant it is that the world has seized on this thought in connection with St. Francis. No prayer so popular as the prayer for peace ascribed to St. Francis and most adequately expressing his inmost soul, though there is no proof of its authenticity.* Rather than St. Francis's peace prayer it is a

ST. FRANCIS PEACE PRAYER

"Lord, make me an instrument of your
        peace.
    where there is hatred, let me sow love;
    where there is injury, pardon;
    where there is doubt, faith;
    where there is despair, hope;
    where there is darkness, light;
    and where there is sadness, joy.

"O Divine Master, grant that I may not
 so much seek
 to be consoled as to console,
 to be understood as to understand,
 to be loved as to love.

"For it is in giving that we receive,
 it is in pardoning that we are pardoned,
 and it is in dying that we are born to
 eternal life."

209. At one time St. Francis wondered whether he should go out into the world at all and not rather spend his time in prayer for the ends he had in view—it was on his resignation as minister general in 1221:

"Brothers, what do you advise and commend? That I give myself wholly to prayer, or that I go about and preach?

"For of course as an insignificant, unlettered person without skill in speech I have received the grace of prayer rather than that of speech. Then too in prayer one seems to win and heap up graces whereas in preaching one as it were distributes the gifts received from Heaven. In prayer there is purification of the interior affections and union with the one true and sovereign Good together with invigoration of virtue; in preaching our spiritual feet pick up dust, we are distracted in many ways, and discipline suffers relaxation. Finally in prayer we address and listen to God, and associate with the angels as if leading an angelic life; in preaching we have to exercise much condescension toward the people and in living among them as people do, we have to think and see and speak and hear things that are human.

"On the other hand, there is one thing that seems to outweigh all this before God, namely that God's only begotten Son, who is the supreme Wisdom, descended from the bosom of the Father for the salvation of souls in order to instruct the world by his example and speak the word of salvation to the people, whom he was both to redeem with the price and cleanse with the bath and nourish with the drink of his sacred Blood, keeping nothing whatever back for himself that he did not give away liberally for our salvation. And since we ought to do everything according to the model of what we see in him as on a high mountain, it seems to be more pleasing to God for me to interrupt my retirement and go out for such work."—B 12.

210. The doubt was settled in favor of his preaching, and one immediate result, as the sources indicate, was the formation of the Third Order of Penitents (LF 16).

Meanwhile, he as well as the brothers had been going forth on their peace errand:*

"Go two by two about the several parts of the world, proclaiming peace to people, and repentance for the forgiveness of their sins. And be patient under trial, assured that the Lord will fulfil his intention and promise. To people who question you give a humble reply, bless those who persecute you, thank those who insult and slander you, because for such things an eternal kingdom is being prepared for us."—1C 29.

211. "While you are proclaiming peace with your lips, be careful to have it even more fully in your heart. Nobody should be roused to wrath or insult on your account. Everyone should rather be moved to peace, goodwill and mercy as a result of your self-restraint.

"For we have been called for the purpose of healing the wounded, binding up those who are bruised, and reclaiming the erring. Many a person may seem to us a child of the Devil that will one day be a disciple of Christ."— LTC 14.

212. The gospel of example meant so much:

"The brothers' way of living in the world ought to be such that, seeing and hearing them everybody will be piously impelled to praise and glorify our Father in Heaven."— LTC 14.

213. "Let us take thought of our vocation. God in his mercy has called us to it not so much for our sake as for the sake of the many.

"So, let us go out into the world and admonish everybody by example as well as word to do penance and be mindful of God's commandments. If you seem feeble and of no importance and wisdom, never fear but preach repentance in a plain way without misgiving, trusting in the Lord, who has overcome the world, since it is he who by the operation of his Spirit speaks through you and in you, in order to admonish all the people to turn to him and keep his commandments.

"You will find some people that have faith, are meek and gracious: they will be happy to welcome you and your words. But you will find far more that have no faith and are proud and blasphemous: they will revile and resist you and set themselves against what you say. Be resolved at heart to bear everything in patience and humility."—LTC 10.

214. But, in fair exchange, the brothers were to be an opportunity for the world's beneficence:

"Go, for in this latest hour the Lesser Brothers have been lent to the world so that the elect may discharge toward them what the Judge is to commend them for: What you have done for the least of my brethren you have done for me."—2C 71.

215. The Lesser Brothers had a special duty to aid the clergy:

"We have been sent as a help to the clergy toward the salvation of souls, so that what they are found less equal to may be supplied by us. Everybody shall have his reward not according to his position but according to his exertion. Understand, brothers, that harvesting souls is highly pleasing to God, and that it can be gained better by peace than by discord with the clergy. Should they interfere with the people's salvation, vengeance belongs to God and he will requite them in time. So, be submissive to those in authority, lest so far as lies in you any spite arise. If you act like children of peace, you will win both clergy and people for the Lord, and the Lord regards that as more acceptable than winning the people only to the scandal of the clergy. Cover up their lapses, supply their, various shortcomings, and when you have done so, be the humbler for it."—2C 146.

216. In his devotion to them and their sacred charge St. Francis once addressed a letter to them on the care of the Blessed Sacrament in those troublous days:

LETTER TO ALL THE CLERGY

Let all of us who are clergymen note the great sin and the ignorance of which some are guilty with regard to the most holy Body and

Blood of our Lord Jesus Christ, as well as the most sacred names and written words which sanctify the body.*

We know that the body cannot be at all unless it be sanctified first by the word. For in this world we have and we see nothing in bodily form of the Most High except his Body and Blood and the names and words through which we have been created and bought back from death to life.

Now, let all who administer mysteries of so very holy a nature, and especially those who minister thoughtlessly, give their careful attention to how wretched are the chalices, corporals and other linens where the Body and Blood of our Lord Jesus Christ is sacrificed. And many leave it in wretched places, and convey it along the way in a regrettable fashion, and receive it unworthily, and administer it to others without due concern.

Then too his names and written words are sometimes trampled under foot, because the sensual man has no appreciation for the things of God (1 Cor. 2, 14).

And all this does not move us with loving concern, though our Lord is loving enough to entrust himself to our hands, and we handle him and receive him on our lips day after day! Do we not know that we are destined to get into his hands?

Well then, let us be quick and determined to do better in these matters and others like them. Wherever the most holy Body of our Lord Jesus Christ may be put away or kept in a way that is not proper, let it be removed from there, to be put away and reserved in a respectable place.

In like manner wherever the names and written words of our Lord are found lying about in dirty places, let them be picked up and put in a decent place, as is proper.

"We know that we are above all bound to observe all these things according to the teaching of our Lord and the decrees of holy Mother Church. Let whoever does not act that way, know that he shall have to give an account of it before our Lord Jesus Christ on the day of judgment.

And let whoever has copies of this writing made in order to get it observed the better, know that he is blest by the Lord.—O 22-23.

217. There was an amount of holy calculation in this wisp of a man who was carried away, blinded, even literally at last, by his all absorbing love of God:

"It is my plan first to convert the prelates through holy humility and reverence. When they notice our holy life and our humble reverence for them, they will ask you to preach to their people to convert them, and they will call their people to hear your

preaching more than your privileges can do
so—which lead you to pride.

"And if you are aloof from all avarice,
and induce the people to render the churches
their due, they will ask you to hear the con-
fessions of their people, though you ought
not to trouble yourselves about that, for if
they are converted they will find confessors
well enough.

"For my part I want just this privilege
from the Lord, never to have any other
privilege from anybody than to do reverence
to everybody and by obedience to the holy
rule to convert everybody by example more
than by word."—MP 50.

218. The bishop was to be their first appeal
when they meant to start a new "place":

"They ought to go to the bishop of the
town and say to him: 'Lord, such and such a
man wants to give us so much ground, for
the love of God and the good of his soul, so
we can build a place there. So we are here to
see you first as the father and lord of the souls
of all the flock committed to you as well as of
our own soul and that of all the brothers who
shall dwell in this place. So with God's
blessing and yours we wish to build there."—
MP 10.

219. And he was never easily rebuffed, as the
bishop of Imola learned when he declared he

could take care of his own people: shown one
door, Francis came back by another:

"My lord, if a father has driven his son
out by one door" (and note the *father* and
son!) "all he can do is come back in by
another door."—2C 147.

220. He preferred that there be no prelacies,
to disturb the brothers' selflessness. In St.
Dominic's presence*, before Cardinal Ugolino,
he pleaded:

"My brothers are called lesser so that they
may not presume to become greater. Their
calling teaches them to keep on the level
ground and follow the footsteps of Christ's
lowliness. That way they shall in due time
be elevated above others in the day when the
saints are requited. If you want them to bear
fruit in the Church of God, keep and preserve
them in the condition of this their calling,
yes bring them back to level ground against
their will.

"I beg you therefore, father, lest they
prove the prouder the poorer they are, and
grow insolent toward the rest, let them by
no means mount to any prelacy."—2C 148.

221. The missions, and martyrdom? That was
different! Gladly he sent them forth. Three times
he made the attempt himself, the third time, at
Damietta in 1219, impressing the sultan where
the crusading army failed. He offered to enter the
ordeal of fire, with the priests of Islam or alone,

if the sultan would accept the Faith: blame his sins if the ordeal failed, acknowledge Christ if it succeeded. But first he warned the reckless Christian hosts of deserved defeat. Said he to his companion:

"The Lord has shown me that if the attack is made that day, it will not go well with the Christians. But if I tell them that, they will consider me a fool; and if I say nothing, I shall not get away from my conscience. What do you advise?"—2C 30.

His companion, Brother Illuminato, advised him to follow his conscience. But the Christians disregarded him to their sorrow. Francis especially lamented the losses of "his brave Spaniards." But he had already determined to go unarmed into the sultan's very camp:

"Trust in the Lord, brother, for the Gospel passage is being fulfilled in us, 'See, I am sending you like sheep into the midst of wolves.'"—B 9.

222. He faced bad situations at home just as courageously. He set the people about Greccio right on the occasion of a visitation:

"For the honor and praise of almighty God, listen to the truth I am declaring to you. If every one of you confesses his sins and does worthy fruits of repentance, I pledge you my word that all this pestilential affliction will go away and that the Lord will have regard for you and multiply your temporal goods.

But listen to this too: I likewise declare to you that if you are ungrateful for his blessings and go back to your vomit, the affliction will be removed, the penalty redoubled, and greater wrath will rage among you."—2C 35.

223. Severe was his indictment of the knights of Perugia, Assisi's olden rival. His warning proved true:

"Listen and understand what the Lord is announcing to you through me his poor servant. And do not say, 'He is from Assisi!' The Lord has exalted you above all your neighbors, and for that you should recognize him the more as your Creator, humbling yourselves not only before God but before your neighbors too.

"Instead, your heart has raised itself up in pride and you have been laying your neighbors waste and killing many of them.

"So, I tell you, unless you change quickly to God's way and render satisfaction to those whom you have injured, the Lord, who lets nothing go unavenged, will for your greater requital, punishment, and disgrace have you rise up one against the other. With sedition and internal war rife, you will suffer greater tribulation than your neighbors could inflict on you."—MP 105. Similarly 2C 37.

224. A similar rebuke he administered on an early occasion to a Roman crowd, with a happier ending:

"I grieve greatly over your wretched state in not only scorning me as a servant of Christ but also despising him in me, because I was telling you about the Redeemer of the world. Now as I leave your city, I invoke him as a witness to your desolation—and he is a faithful witness. Now for your confusion I am going to preach Christ's gospel to the brute animals and the birds of the sky, that hearing the saving words of God, they may obey and comply."—CRW.

225. Like so many of his unlettered sons through the centuries, Francis was sought, and now and then tested, for his deeper wisdom, as when a Dominican at Siena asked him to explain, for his peace of conscience, the passage of Ezechiel 3, 18, If you do not denounce his wickedness to the godless person, I will demand his soul at your hand:

"Insofar as the passage must be applied generally, I take it to mean that the servant of God ought to be so aflame in his personal life and holiness as to reprove all the wicked by the light of his example and the tongue of his association with others. In that way, I say, the luster of his life and the fragrance of his good name will denounce their wickedness to everybody."—2C 103.

226. He "had a way" with people. He made two pleas to a certain man who would not forgive his master. The first failed, the second worked:

"Brother, forgive your master for the love of God, to set your soul free, and it may be your master will give back what he is withholding from you. Otherwise you will have lost both your goods and your soul."

"See here, I am giving you this mantle, and I beg you to pardon your master for the love of the Lord God."—2C 89.

227. Parents who had given a son to the order became "ours":

"Can we give some kind of alms to our mother? Give our mother this New Testament. She can sell it for her need, for we are directed in it to help the poor. At that I believe the gift of it will please God more than the reading of it."—2C 91.

228. He could tease. Even at the last when the knights were conveying him on his last journey home to St. Mary's he twitted them to try his way of begging when their "flies," as he called money, failed to buy food. It worked too:

"You are getting nothing because you rely on your flies more than on God. Go back over the round of houses you have made and humbly ask for alms, offering the people the love of God instead of money. Do not be ashamed, for since the Fall everything is granted to us as an alms, and the great Almoner in his gentle pity is bountiful to the worthy and the unworthy alike."—2C 77.

229. High and low came under his thoughtful ministration. When he could not reach them personally, he had letters multiplied and sent to them. He would have public officials think of grace rather than of what we call graft. Hence his

LETTER TO PUBLIC OFFICIALS

To all magistrates and consuls, judges and governors all over the world, and to all whom this letter may reach:

Brother Francis, your lowly little servant in the Lord God, wishes you health and peace.

Take note and reflect that the day of death is approaching. So I ask you with whatever reverence I can that you do not let the cares and worries of this world which you have, cause you to forget God and turn from the path of his commandments, because all those who forget him and turn away from his commandments are under a curse (Ps. 118, 21) and shall be consigned by him to oblivion (Ezech. 33, 13). And when their day of death arrives, everything they thought they had shall be taken from them (Lk. 8, 18). And the greater their wisdom and power was in the world, the greater will be their torment in Hell (Wis. 6, 7).

For that reason I advise you strongly, my lords, to think less of all such care and worry, and lovingly to receive the most holy Body and Blood of our Lord Jesus Christ in holy memory of him. And do the Lord so much honor among the people entrusted to you that every evening you have a crier or some other signal summon all your people to render praise and thanksgiving to the almighty Lord God. If you do not act thus, it is well for you to know that you must render an account before your Lord Jesus Christ on the day of judgment.

Let those who keep this writing about their person and observe it, know that they shall be blest by the Lord God.—O 111-112.

230. Replete with more than earthly wisdom, and closing with the graphic deathbed scene of the impenitent, procrastinating holder of ill-gotten goods, is the Letter to all the Faithful. It has been regarded by some authorities as the most original form of a rule for people living in the world (third order):

LETTER TO ALL THE FAITHFUL

To all Christians, religious, clerics, and lay men and women, to all people living all over the world, Brother Francis, their servant and subject, bids reverent homage, true peace from above and sincere charity in the Lord:

"Since I am the servant of all, I am obliged to serve them all and communicate to them the fragrant words of my Lord. So, with the thought in mind that due to my weak and feeble body I cannot visit you all

singly in person, I resolved with this present
letter and message to convey to you the
words of our Lord, Jesus Christ, who is the
Word of the Father, and the words of the
Holy Ghost, which are spirit and life (Jn.
6, 64).

230a. The most high Father announced
through his holy archangel Gabriel to the
holy and glorious Virgin Mary that this
Word of the Father, so worthy of reverence,
so holy and glorious, was coming down from
Heaven, and from her womb he took on the
true flesh of our frail human nature. And he,
though he was rich (2 Cor. 8, 9) above all
things, nonetheless wished with his most
blessed Mother to take poverty as his choice.

With his suffering near, he celebrated the
Passover with his disciples, and taking bread,
he gave thanks and blessed it and broke it,
saying: Take and eat, this is my body. And
taking the chalice he said: This is my blood
of the new testament, which shall be shed for
you and for many for the remission of your
sins. (cf. Mt. 26, 26; Lk. 22, 19; 1 Cor. 11,
24.) Later he prayed to his Father, saying:
Father, if it can be done, let this chalice pass
from me (Mt. 26, 39). And his sweat became
like drops of blood dripping down on the
ground (Lk. 22, 44). Still he placed his will
in the will of his Father, saying: Father, your

will be done; not as I wish, but as you wish (Mt. 26-39 and 42).

230b. Now, such was the will of his Father that his glorious blest Son, whom he gave up to us and who was born for us, should offer himself up in his own blood as a sacrifice and victim on the altar of the cross, not for himself, through whom all things have been made (Jn. 1, 3), but for our sins, leaving us an example, so that we might follow in his footsteps (1 Peter 2, 21). It is his will that we all should be saved by him and receive him with a pure heart and a chaste body. But there are few who care to receive him and be saved by him, though his yoke is sweet and his burden light (Mt. 11, 30).

230c. Those who have not the will to taste how sweet the Lord is (Ps. 33, 9) and who love the darkness more than the light (Jn. 3, 19), being unwilling to fulfil God's commandments, are under a curse. It is said of them by the prophet: Cursed are they who turn away from your commandments (Ps. 118, 21). But oh, how blessed and blest are they who love the Lord and do as the Lord himself says in the Gospel: You shall love the Lord your God with all your heart and all your soul, and your neighbor as yourself (Mt. 22, 37).

So let us love God and adore him with a

clean heart and mind, because that is what
he desires above all when he says: The true
worshipers will worship the Father in spirit
and in truth (Jn. 4, 23). For all who worship
him, should worship him in the spirit of
truth (ib. 24). Let us speak his praise and
pray to him day and night with the words,
Our Father, who are in Heaven, for we should
pray always and never lose heart (Lk. 18, 1)

230d. We should, in particular, confess
all our sins to the priest and receive from him
the Body and Blood of our Lord Jesus Christ.
Whoever does not eat his flesh and drink his
blood cannot enter the kingdom of God. Let
him of course eat and drink worthily, because
whoever receives unworthily, eats and drinks
judgment on himself, not distinguishing the
body of our Lord (1 Cor. 11, 29)—that is, not
distinguishing it from other foods.

Moreover, let us produce worthy fruits of
repentance (Lk. 3, 8). And let us love our
neighbors like ourselves, and if there is
anyone that has not the inclination or the
strength to love them like himself, at least
let him not bring evil on them but do good
to them.

230e. Such, however, as have received the
power of judgment over others, should exercise judgment with mercy, just as they wish
to get mercy from the Lord. For judgment

without mercy will be done to him who does no mercy (Jas. 2, 13). So, let us have charity and humility, and give alms, because they wash souls from the grime of sins (cf. Tob. 4, 11). For people lose everything they leave in this world, but they do take with them the reward of their charity and the alms they have given, for which they will have their reward and fitting recompense from the Lord.

230f. We must also fast and abstain from vice and sin (cf. Ecclus. 3, 32) as well as from excess in food and drink, and we must be Catholic. We must likewise visit the churches often and be respectful to the clergy not only for their sake, if they are sinners, but for their charge and ministry of the most holy Body and Blood of our Lord Jesus Christ, which they sacrifice on the altar and receive and distribute to others. And let us all be firmly convinced that no one can be saved except through the Blood of our Lord Jesus Christ and the holy words of our Lord, which the clergy repeat and announce and minister to us, and which it is for them alone to administer, and for nobody else.

But the religious, who have renounced the world, are especially bound to do more and greater things, but without neglecting other matters (Lk. 11, 42).

230g. We must hate our person with its vices and sins, because our Lord says in the

Gospel that all vices and sins come forth from our heart (Mt. 15, 18). We must love our enemies and do good to those who hate us (Lk. 6, 27). We must observe the commandments and counsels of our Lord Jesus Christ.

We must deny ourselves and place our person under the yoke of service and holy obedience, as everyone of us has promised the Lord. And no man be bound in obedience to obey anybody in a matter where sin or fault is committed.

230h. Let any person, however, who is entrusted with the obedience of others and who is regarded as someone greater, become like someone lesser (Lk. 22, 26) and like the servant of the rest of the brethren, and let him have, and show his several brethren, the mercy he would wish to have done to himself in any similar case. And let him not get angry with a brother over the offense of a brother, but kindly admonish him and bear with him with all patience and humility.

230i. We must not be wise and prudent according to the flesh (1 Cor. 1, 26), but rather be simple, humble and pure. And let us regard our person with shame and contempt, because all of us through our own fault are wretched and rank, and foul as vermin, as our Lord says by the prophet: I am a worm and no man, a thing men revile and the people spurn (Ps. 21, 7). And never should we desire to be above others, but we should rather be their servants and subject to every human creature for God's sake (1 Peter 2, 13).

230j. And all who act thus and persevere to the end—the Spirit of the Lord shall rest on them (Is. 11, 2) and make his home and abode in them (Jn. 14, 23), and they shall be children of the heavenly Father (Mt. 5, 45), whose work they do, and they are the spouses, brothers and mothers of our Lord Jesus Christ. We are his spouses when through the Holy Ghost the faithful soul is united with Jesus Christ. We are his brothers when we do the will of his Father, who is in Heaven (Mt. 12, 50). We are his mothers when we carry him about in our heart and person by means of love and a clean and sincere conscience, and we give birth to him by means of our holy actions, which should shine as an example to others.

230k. Oh, what a glorious, holy and great thing it is to have a Father in Heaven! How holy, fair and lovable to have a Spouse in Heaven! How holy it is, and how choice, gratifying and helpful to humility, how peaceful, sweet, lovable and of all things desirable to have a Brother like that, who gave his life for his sheep (Jn. 10, 15) and prayed to the Father for us with the words: "Holy Father, in your name keep those whom you have given me. Father, all those whom you gave me in the world, were yours and you gave them to me. And the words you have given me, I have given to them. And they have received them and have known truly that I have come forth from you, and they have believed that you have sent me. I am praying for them, not for the world: Bless and sanctify them. And for them I sanctify myself, that they may be sanctified in their unity, just as we are. And, Father, I wish that where I am, they also may be with me, that they may see my splendor in your kingdom" (cf. Jn. 17, 6-24).

230L. And because he has suffered so much for us and has done and will in future do so much good to us, let every creature in Heaven and on earth and in the sea and its depths render God praise, glory, honor and blessing, for he is our strength and power, who alone is good, alone the most high, alone almighty and admirable, alone glorious and holy, praiseworthy and blest without end forevermore. Amen.

230m. All they, however, who are not repentant and do not receive the Body and Blood of our Lord Jesus Christ but commit vice and sin, walking the way of their evil appetites and desires; who do not observe what they have promised; who with their person serve the world, their fleshly desires, and the cares and worries of this world, while with their mind they serve the Devil, deceived by him whose children they are and whose work they do: all such are blind, since they do not see the true light, our Lord Jesus Christ. They have no wisdom spiritually, because they do not have the Son of God in them, who is the true wisdom of the Father, and it is said of them: Their wisdom has been swallowed up (Ps. 106, 27). They see the truth, acknowledge it, know it, and yet commit evil and knowingly lose their soul.

230n. Look to yourselves, you blind people, deceived by your enemies, that is, by the flesh, the world and the Devil. For to the body it is sweet to commit sin but bitter to serve God, because all vice and sin come forth and proceed from the heart of a man, as is said in the Gospel.

230o. And there is nothing good for you neither in this world nor in the next. You think you are going to keep these worldly vanities a long time, but you are deceived, because the day and the hour will come of which you neither think, nor know, nor notice anything. The body begins to fail, death approaches, relatives and friends come and say, Arrange your affairs. Wife and children, kin and friends pretend to weep. Looking about, the person sees them weeping and is moved by an evil impulse, and thinks and says: See here, I place my soul and body and all I have in your hands. Indeed, a man like that is cursed for entrusting and risking his soul and body and all he has in such hands. For that reason the Lord says by the prophet: Cursed the man that places his reliance in man (Jer. 17, 5).

Directly they have the priest come. And the priest says to him: Are you willing to undertake penance for all your sins? He answers, I am. Are you willing to make satisfaction out of your property so far as you can in matters where you have done wrong and defrauded and cheated people? And he replies, No. And the priest says: Why not?—Because I have left everything in the hands of my kin and friends! And then he begins to lose his speech, and so the wretched man dies a bitter death.

230p. But let everybody realize that no matter where or how a person dies in guilt and sin without due satisfaction, when he can make satisfaction and does not do so, the Devil snatches his soul from his body amid anguish and distress such as only the victim of it can understand. And whatever talent and power, knowledge and wisdom he believed he had, will be taken from him (cf. Lk. 8, 18). And his kin and friends take over his property and divide it up, and say later on: Cursed be his soul, he could have acquired a lot more to give us than he did. But the worms devour his body. Thus he loses soul and body in this short life, and goes to Hell, there to be tormented without end.

In the name of Father and of the Son and of the Holy Ghost. Amen.

230q. All whom this letter may reach, I, Brother Francis, your lesser servant, ask and entreat, in the charity which is God (1 Jn. 4, 16) and with the desire to kiss your feet, that you feel obliged to accept these fragrant words of our Lord Jesus Christ with humility and charity, and to fulfil them graciously and observe them perfectly. Let those who cannot read, have them read often and keep them on their person while practicing them conscientiously to the last, for they are spirit and life. And those who do not act so, shall give an account for it on judgment day at the tribunal of Christ. All, both men and women, who accept them kindly and understand them and send copies to others, shall, if they persevere to the end in them, be blest by Father and Son and Holy Ghost. Amen. (O. 87-98).

Part IX

Saint Francis
Addresses himself
to the
Creature World

PART IX

St. Francis addresses himself to the creature world above, on earth, below

God the Father, Jesus Christ the Son, the Holy Ghost the Paraclete: one to whom the blessed Trinity was as close as it was to Francis, would find his loving way to the Blessed Virgin Mother of God. What Francis did and what he said was redolent of Mary, from his beginning at St. Mary's of the Angels through all the fortunes of Lady Poverty to his going home, at the same Little Portion where he began.

231. Deep with mystical comprehension is his

SALUTE TO THE BLESSED VIRGIN

"Hail, holy Lady! Most holy Queen!
    Mary, Mother of God, yet a virgin
      forever!
Chosen by the most high holy Father in
    Heaven, and by him with his most holy
    beloved Son and the Spirit Paraclete
    consecrated!—
You in whom there was and there is all
    the fulness of grace and everything good!

"Hail, his palace! Hail, his tabernacle!
Hail, his home! Hail, his vesture!
Hail, his handmaiden! Hail, his mother!
And hail, too, all you holy virtues, which
by the grace and light of the Holy Ghost
are infused into the hearts of the faithful,
to make of the faithless faithful children
of God."—O 123.

232. Again and again he repeated the anthem
of the Office of the Passion:

"Holy Virgin Mary, there was never anyone like you born in the world among women!
Daughter and handmaiden of the most high
King, our Father in Heaven. Mother of our
most holy Lord Jesus Christ. Spouse of the
Holy Ghost! With the archangel St. Michael,
and all the Virtues of Heaven, and all the
saints, pray for us at the throne of your
beloved most holy Son, our Lord and Master."

233. Still another prayer, ascribed to him*:

"O holy Mother, sweet and fair to see, for
us beseech the King, your dearest Son,
our Lord Jesus Christ, to death for us
delivered:

That in his pitying clemency, and by virtue of his most holy Incarnation, and
bitter death

He may pardon our sins. Amen."

234. Also his in idea and spirit if not in fact is:

"Oh, our glorious sovereign Lady and our
   hope!
Just as the world received its Savior at
   your hands,
So at your hands do I hope once to see my
   Lord Jesus Christ. Amen."

235. The happiness of Francis in his fellow men and his loving power over them we have had occasion to see.

Numerous too are the passages that could be quoted as to his relation to the lower creatures. They culminate in *The Canticle of Brother Sun* **271, 281.**

Proverbial is his relation to the animal kingdom and his address to it. Birds were favorites:

"My brother birds, you ought to praise your Creator mightily, and always love him. He has given you feathers to wear, and wings to fly, and whatever you have need of. God has made you noble among his creatures, and given you your home in the pure air, and though you neither sow nor reap, still without any trouble to you he protects and governs you."—1C 58.

236. Of La Verna, where he was presently to have the Stigmata, he said:

"I believe our Lord Jesus Christ is pleased to have us stay on this solitary mountain, since our little brother and sister birds show such joy at our coming."—LF 1st Stigm.

237. He could shame man with the animal world. Thus at Rome (see **224**):

"Now for your confusion I am going to preach Christ's Gospel to the brute animals and the birds of the sky, that hearing the saving words of God, they may obey and comply. I bid you," said he, "in the name of Jesus Christ whom the Jews crucified and whose preaching these pitiable people of Rome have despised, to come here to me and hear the word of God in the name of Him who created you and delivered you from the waters of the deluge in the days of Noe."— CRW.

238. At Alviano he had some rivalry to contend with in uttering God's praises:

"My sister swallows, it is time now for me to speak too, for up till now you have talked enough. Now you hear the word of God and remain silent and quiet until the word of the Lord has been taken care of."—1C 59.

238a. Doves reminded him of lovable virtues:

"Good lad, please give me those harmless birds, emblems in Scripture of humble, pure, and faithful souls; they must not get into ruthless hands that will kill them."—LF 22.

239. The lark was a prime favorite: it sang its way so merrily right up into the heavens. They were to have special care on Christmas day (see above **82**), and one thing he would urge on the emperor if ever he got speech with him was that "for the love of God and myself he make a special law that nobody is to trap or kill our sister larks, or do them any harm."—MP 114.

240. Besides, was not sister lark a good religious?

"Sister lark has a cowl like religious have, and a humble bird she is. She is happy going along the road to find a few kernels for herself. Even if she must find them amid dung, she picks them out and eats them. She praises the Lord very sweetly in her flight, like good religious, who spurn the earth, whose conversation is always in the heavens, and whose mind is always on the praises of God. Her garment, to wit her feathers, resemble the ground, and she gives the religious an example not to wear choice and showy garments but such as are plain in price and color, just as the ground is plainer than the rest of the elements."—MP 113.

241. All the creature world down to the least insect and even inanimate nature was somehow a reminder of Divine truth to him. They cried out to him:

"God made me for you, O man!"—MP 118.

"Notice that sheep there walking along so meek among those goats and their does: I tell you it was like that our Lord Jesus Christ went about meek and lowly among the

Pharisees and chief priests. I beg you therefore, son, to have pity on this poor little
sheep with me for love of Him. Let us pay
the price and lead her away from among
these goats."—1C 77.

242. "Why are you torturing these my
brother lambs, trussing and hanging them up
that way?"

When told they were for the market and
slaughter:

"Oh, no, not that! Take this mantle I am
wearing in payment and give me the lambs."
—1C 79.

243. Animals came at call, even when they
had reason to fear man:

"Little brother rabbit, come here to me.
Why did you let yourself be trapped that
way?"—1C 60.

244. And all the world knows the story of the
bad wolf, who was no worse than many a bad
man, tamed by Francis of his murdering ways
(LF 21).

245. Lifeless creatures shared his reverence.
When he strewed ashes on his food to curb his
taste, he remarked simply:

"Brother ash is pure."—LTC 5.

245a. Hot, thirsty, way-worn, he and sensitive
Brother Masseo sit down at a stone by a roadside
spring to eat their beggarly crusts. Francis speaks

of a treasure while Masseo finds little human comfort. Francis says:

"That is just why I regard this as so great a treasure, because man has had no hand in it. Everything has been arranged for us by God's providence, plain to see in this fountain so clear, this beautiful stone table, and this bread of charity. So, do let us beg God to help us love the treasure of holy poverty with all our heart."—LF 13.

246. He reveled in brother fire, almost literally at the test he proposed to the sultan (see **221** above). He forgot his courtesy to brother fire one day when his wattle hut burned and he snatched his burning coverlet from the flame. In amends:

"I will not have this pelt over me again, because due to my avarice I would not let brother fire eat it."—MP 117.

247. He thanked God for brothers sun and fire:

"In the morning when the sun rises, everybody ought to praise God, who created the sun for our benefit; through it our eyes get the light in daytime. At night, when darkness falls, everybody ought to praise God because of brother fire, through whom our eyes get light at night time.

"For all of us are as it were blind, and the Lord with these two brothers of ours gives light to our eyes. Because of them in particular, and all the creatures we make use of day

by day, we ought to praise the Creator."—
MP 119.

248. Brother fire returned the courtesy when
Francis underwent that cruel temple cauteriza-
tion for his eyes:

"My brother fire, that you might rival the
beauty of all other things, the Most High
created you vigorous, fair and useful. Be
gracious to me at this moment, be courteous,
for of old have I loved you in the Lord. I beg
the great Lord, who created you, to temper
your heat now, so that it will burn me gently
enough to bear it."

The brothers fled when the doctor laid the iron
on. Francis teased when they returned:

"You with your faint spirits and weak
hearts! What made you run away? I tell you
candidly, I neither felt the heat of the fire nor
any pain in my flesh."

Teasing still, he turned to the doctor:

"If the flesh is not seared well, lay the iron
on again!"—2C 166.

246. Heaven and earth, where Mary is queen,
and the demons below, whom Mary curbs by
special commission from God! Evidently Mary
sometimes passes the charge on. When possessed
people were brought to Francis and the demon
would not get out promptly, Francis called for
guileless, humble Brother Juniper, and it worked.

"Unless you leave this creature on the instant, I will call Brother Juniper here."—LF Life of Bl. Juniper 2.

247. Usually only the word of Francis was needed, as at San Gemini:

"Brother, let us pray to the Lord for this woman, that for his honor and glory God may strike the yoke of the devil from her . . . In the name of our Lord Jesus Christ I command you, demon, under obedience to leave her and never dare to get in her way again."—1C 69.

248. "I saw the devil perched on the back of that disobedient brother, holding him tight at the neck. In that rider's power he disregarded the bridle of obedience and followed the reins of what that one inspired. When I began beseeching the Lord for the brother, the demon sped on his way in confusion."—2C 34.

249. Francis was not spared vexation by the evil spirits. He said one time:

"If my brothers knew how numerous and great are the trials and afflictions the devils cause me, not one of them but would be moved to compassion and pity."—MP 99.

250. He took it all as under the eye of God:

"Evil one, you can brandish your weapons

against me here to no more effect than if we were out in public in sight of everybody."—1C 72.

251. "Do your worst, false, spiteful spirits! You are powerless except insofar as the Hand from above eases its control. For my part, I stand here ready to endure with all contentment whatever that Hand may decide to inflict."—B 10.

252. "I see this devil is quite shrewd. Unable to hurt my soul, he is resolved to prevent what my body needs, so that I cannot sleep or keep upright at prayer. Interfering with my devotion and gladness of heart that way, he would get me to complain about my ailment."—MP 98.

They had induced him to use a pillow in illness that night. He looked on it as a punishment for softness:

"Brother, I have not been able to sleep tonight nor keep upright to pray. My head is swimming, my knees are shaking, and all my bodily frame is quaking as if I had eaten darnel bread. I believe the Devil is in that pillow at my head. Take it away!"—2C 64.

Part X

Saint Francis
Meets
an Emergency

PART X
St. Francis meets an emergency

253. At this point we reach an issue which has caused critics and so-called experts to do great damage to the holy glory of St. Francis, unintentionally to an extent, but nevertheless factually.* Briefly the facts are as follows:

In the years from 1209 to 1220 the order of St. Francis grew, grew fast, grew too fast for due assimilation by all the followers of so spiritual an ideal as that of St. Francis, which was nothing less than total immolation of self to God and his love and his cause. For to Francis, Lady Poverty meant nothing less than that—something far beyond the narrow bounds of mere material poverty.

There was above all a looseness of organization, inherent in the early rule with the freedom of movement practiced by Francis and his genuine followers, that was bound to lay the order open to scandal and certainly obloquy where the true all-out self-dedication of St. Francis was not appreciated.

There arose the dilemma: on one hand, save the spiritual utterness of expropriation in the ideal of St. Francis; on the other hand, curb the vagaries

—in the case one may almost say the vagrancy.

Many in number, diversified in nationality, scattered geographically as were the sons of Francis by this time, you could not help offending also well-meaning, otherwise holy men on both sides by almost any measure you took. Not even necessarily brief total chapters, like that of the Mats, could obviate that difficulty.

There must be a measure of hard and fast universal discipline—and local material living conditions under which such discipline could be enforced. Going and coming almost at will, the "working out" at that time customary in the order, also going off into hermitages when the spirit, good, bad or indifferent, moved—such things had to be drastically restricted, brought to common rule; for to make exceptions freely was to undo the entire sanction.

Bigger if not imposing and luxuriously appointed places or friaries were definitely indicated —but in providing them you might go too far; or you might keep within reasonable holy limits and still be accused of going too far; also by well-meaning men.

Again, on the enforcement side, you might go too far and believe all individuality had to merge in rigid monastic discipline as far as it was characteristic of the ancient orders. Then you no longer had Francis's ideal of the Order of Friars Minor.

The result of these and similar problems? A splitting of opinions and tendencies, which, aided by the only too human whisperings, the "detraction," that go with it, can soon disrupt the holiest organization unless a firm hand is taken, a hand if anything more realistic than idealistic, in effect if not in deep-down intention.

253a. Where did Francis stand? Wherever and on whatever else he stood, Francis stood, in his writings as well as his spoken words and no less his actions—Francis stood, I say, on authority, solidly, even vehemently, first and last: the authority of the Holy See (see Note **210**) as then represented by Pope Honorius III and the Cardinal Protector appointed by Pope Honorius, that Cardinal Protector being Ugolino, who soon after Francis died was to be Pope Gregory IX; and the authority of the Vicar, later Minister, General of the order, on down through the Minister Provincial to the local Guardian, "in whose hands I wish to be so much a captive that I cannot go about or do anything against his orders and his will, for he is my master" (**282f**).

253b. Where did Francis stand? First and last at the side of Lady Poverty. But she was to him, in his Seraphic mysticism, more than a penniless beggar lady however beautiful: she was his ideal of utter selflessness and self-immolation for the love and service of God.

And whatever stand we take, let it be taken with these two points of orientation in view: Francis's unfaltering reverence for the authorities of the Church and of the order; and Francis's equally unfaltering, constantly growing, spirit of self-immolation—a thing of course which only genuine mysticism can understand.

Let us not rob Seraphic St. Francis of these

two crowning glories of his Christlike life.

Let us fit the rest of his life, especially the last six years of his life, into these two indisputable facts. The rest is debatable, controversial, where it is not, in the light of these two facts, just plain fatuous.

The facts give us a picture of Francis in these years as at the peak of spiritual happiness, which culminated in his triumphant *Canticle of Brother Sun* just before he went home to God in 1226, after God had come down to him on La Verna's heights in 1224. In 1223, at Christmas time, Francis is in Rome, where the final rule he drafted is being approved by the Pope on November 29. Shortly after he is sending word from Rome to John Velita of Greccio, happy as a child about the privilege he had just received from the Pope of celebrating his famous Crib devotion.

253c. After all it was his rule which he saw solemnly approved in 1223. And in that rule it is that he says:

"I enjoin on the ministers by obedience that they ask of the Lord Pope one of the cardinals of the holy Roman Church to be governor, protector, and corrector of this brotherhood: so that, *submissive and subject always at the feet of the same holy Church, grounded in the Catholic Faith,*" (italics this author's), "we may, as we have firmly promised, observe the poverty and the humility and the holy Gospel of our Lord Jesus Christ."

Whichever way we look, there is no disgruntled, sulking Francis, at odds with the Church and the order. Flashes of impatience, of anger if you will, but at that, against which side, against whom, for what? But habitually? Even against the worst offender? That was not the way of Francis. That is not what the facts say, not what his words say.

254. Francis realized early in this period that something was amiss. As a first measure of redress he hit on the expedient of a special cardinal—he opted Cardinal Ugolino—to look after the interests of the order and defend it against the annoyance of detraction (1217). It was not in any gloomy mood! On the contrary: the half-humorous vision in sleep of a luckless black hen trying in vain to get her large brood of wayward chicks under her wings, gave shape to the thought:

"I am this hen, small in size, black in guise, who needs to be served by dovelike simplicity coupled with innocence of life; for, most rare as that is on earth, yet it flies untrammeled right up to heaven.

"The chicks are the brothers, multiplied in number and grace, whom it is not in the power of Francis to defend against annoyance from the people and the detraction of their tongues.

"So I will go and commend them to the holy Roman Church, that by the rod of her authority the evil-minded may be cowed and the children of God, to the promotion of eternal salvation, may enjoy full freedom everywhere. In that way her children will recognize their mother's dear blessings and will always with special attachment cleave close to her reverend footsteps. With her protection there will be no evil chance in the order and the son of Belial will not transgress unpunished on the vineyard of the Lord.

"Holy as she is, she will watch jealously over the glory of our poverty, and will not allow our good reputation for lowliness to be dimmed by the mists of pride. She will maintain unharmed among us the bonds of charity and peace, striking dissenters with her severest censure. Under her glance the holy observance of Gospel purity will flourish continuously, and she will not suffer the fragrance of our life to evaporate even for an hour."—2C 24.

Then, before Honorius III:

"My lord, as you know, approach to majesty as great as yours is not easily granted to men who are poor and of no regard. You hold the world in your hands, and affairs of unusually great business do not permit you to attend to very little matters. For that reason, my lord, I request of Your Holiness's kind-heartedness that this lord of Ostia be conceded to us as our pope, so that, always saving the dignity of your preeminence, the brothers may in time of need have recourse to him and enjoy at his hand the benefits of both protection and guidance."—2C 25.

255. For the next several years Francis so to say lived at Cardinal Ugolino's doorstep. Interesting it is to know that he addressed him as "Bishop of the whole world" (1C 100).

But never did Francis cease warning the brothers. We have seen it in his warnings to superiors against "detractors" in the order (**200**). We see it in the following passages against breaking faith with the public:

"To the extent the brothers turn away from poverty, the world will turn away from them, and they will seek and not find. But if they cling to my Lady Poverty, the world will support them, because they have been given to the world for its salvation."

"There is an understanding between the world and the brothers: The latter owe the world a good example, the world owes them provision for their needs. If belying their trust they withdraw their good example, the world in just reproof withdraws its hand."

"Oh, that it might happen—it will happen, I say—that because of very rarely noticing Friars Minor about, the world will wonder at their fewness!"—2C 70.

256. The next step was that, feeling himself no longer adequate, Francis voluntarily resigned in favor of a vicar general within a year:

"Henceforth I am dead to you. But here is Brother Peter Cattaneo, and let me and all of you obey him."

"I commend to you, O Lord, the family you have hitherto committed to me, and now, no longer able to take care of it because of my infirmities, of which you know, dearest Lord, I commend it to the ministers. Let them be bound to render an account before you, O Lord, on the day of judgment if any brother perish through their negligence or example or even harsh correction."—2C 143.

257. Yet, hold to the ideal of our way of life — we need not take up the monastic way:

"My brothers, my brothers! God has called me along a path of humility and has shown me a way of simplicity. I want you not to name me any rule, neither of St. Augustine, nor of St. Bernard, nor of St. Benedict.

"The Lord said I was to be a new kind of fool in the world, and God did not want to lead me along any other road but by that knowledge. But God will put you to shame through your learning and wisdom.

"For my part I rely on the bailiffs of the Lord, that he will punish you through them and that for that purpose you will return willy-nilly to your proper state, to your reproach."—Legenda Antiqua.

258. In that sense we are to understand his

righteous impatience with stampeded innovators who were "snatching his order out of his hands," believing the ancient rules were the only salvation. There was no thought in it of going back on his abdication:

"I love the brothers as much as I can. But if they followed my footsteps, I should really love them still more and not estrange myself from them. For there are among the superiors some who are dragging them in other directions, putting the example of the ancients before them and giving too little heed to my instructions. What they are doing will be clear later on."

"Who are these men who have snatched my order and that of my brothers out of my hands? If I get to the general chapter, I will show them the nature of my will."

Yet no thought of forgetting his accepted place and of deposing such ministers:

"Let them live as they please, for there is less harm in the loss of a few than of many." —2C 188.

259. To Francis, his was the place of a dutiful religious, given wholly to the pleasure of God. In that attitude, as even the *Mirror of Perfection* tells, God comforted and confirmed him, so that Francis said:

"I have sworn and determined to keep the just ways of the Lord and to observe the rule

which the Lord gave me and those desirous
of following me. For the brothers too have
obligated themselves to that, just as I.

"Therefore, after abdicating my office on
account of my infirmities and other reasonable grounds, I am obliged henceforth to do
no more than pray for the order and give the
brothers a good example. *For this assurance I
have had of the Lord and know to be true that even if
infirmity did not excuse me, the greatest help I can
give my order is daily to spend my time praying for
it, so that the Lord may govern, preserve and protect
it. To this I have bound myself to the Lord and to the
brothers that if any of the brothers perishes through
my bad example, I am willing to be bound to render
account for him to the Lord.*"

Wherefore, if any brother ever told him he
ought to take a hand in the government of the
order, he replied:

"Since the brothers know what they ought
to do and what to avoid, there is nothing
further for me to do but teach them by my
actions, because that is the purpose for which
I have been given them in life and after
death."—MP 81.

260. We quote a last passage on the emer-
gency, likewise taken from the *Mirror of Perfection.* It shows graphically what Francis's reaction
was when anybody suggested that he take a hand
at correction after his abdication:

"The Lord pardon you, brother, for wanting to cross and antagonize me by involving

me in matters which are none of my business. As long as I held the office of superiority over the brothers and they kept to their vocation and profession, ailing as I always was from the beginning of my conversion, with small trouble to myself I satisfied them with my example and preaching.

"But when I saw that the Lord multiplied the numbers of the brothers and that in their lukewarm lack of the spirit they began to depart from the right and safe way which they used to walk; that treading the wider path which leads to death they paid no attention to their vocation and profession and to good example; that they were not minded to quit the dangerous, deadly road they had taken, on my preaching and direction and the continued good example I had been showing them: therefore I commended the superiorship and government of the order to the Lord and to the ministers.

"Now, though at the time I renounced the office of the superiorship over the brothers I excused myself before the brothers in the general chapter on the grounds that because of my infirmities I was not able to keep charge of them, still, had the brothers been willing to live according to my will, I would then for their comfort and benefit not have wished they should have any other minister but myself to the day of my death.

"For when a good, loyal subject knows and observes the will of his prelate, the prelate need have little enough worry concerning him. Yes, I would be so happy at the goodness of the brothers for their gain and my gain that if I lay ill in bed, I would not pause to comply with them; because my office, that is the office of superiorship, is purely spiritual, that is, it consists in controlling vice and correcting and amending it by spiritual means. If I cannot correct and amend it by preaching, direction and example, I am not going to be an executioner to punish and flog them, like the authorities of this world."

"For I have this confidence in the Lord that invisible foes, they who are the Lord's bailiffs to administer punishment in this world and the next, will yet take vengeance on those who transgress God's commandments and the vow they have professed, and will see that they get their correction from people out in the world to their shame and disgrace, and so they will return to their vocation and profession.

"To my dying day, however, I will not cease at least by example and good endeavor to teach the brothers how to tread the course the Lord has shown me, the course I have till now by word and example, taught and shown them, so that they are inexcusable before the Lord and I am not bound further

to render an account for them before God."—
MP 71.

Francis lived as great saints live. Francis died
as great saints die. Only, to St. Francis it was
given to die with a burst of immortal song on his
lips, which mingled with the eternal chants of the
blessed in Heaven. Indeed, such were the mystic
heights to which he attained in ascending the
mount of complete immolation that it is hard to
say from which perspective he latterly viewed the
things of this world: from that of man on earth or
that of the blessed choirs above.

260a. But one of his last formal wishes as to
the brothers, in April 1226, was (**269**):

"That they do always remain loyal and
submissive to the prelates and all the clergy
of the holy Roman Church."—MP 88.

Part XI

Saint Francis
Addresses himself
to Brother Death

PART XI

St. Francis addresses himself to Brother Death*

261. This is story of the final blessed days of
St. Francis on earth:

In November 1223 solemn approval is given to
the last rule he wrote.

On Christmas day 1223 the Crib scene at
Greccio is enacted.

At Pentecost 1224 the general chapter is held
in which his last rule is proclaimed; he did not
attend.

In September 1224 he receives the Stigmata on
Mt. La Verna.

In summer 1225, with his infirmities gathering,
at St. Damian's in Assisi, he composes the initial
stanzas of *The Canticle of Brother Sun*.

In September 1225 he journeys to Rieti to the
oculist. In March 1226 he is with the physician
at Siena.

Then he is carried back through Cortona and
Bagnorea to Assisi, where Doctor Buongiovanni
applies the cautery and tells Francis of his im-
pending death.

At Assisi the Pardon and the Death stanzas of
the Canticle are composed.

Then out home at long last to St. Mary of the

Angels: under Mary's patronage his Seraphic life began and under Mary's patronage it was to end October 4, 1226. His (large) Testament is written at this time.

Anywhere, any time along the road, we might hear Francis say what he was wont to say in cheer:

"Brothers, let us begin to serve God our Lord, for up till now we have made little or no progress."—1C 103.

262. The holy transports of the Christmas scene at Greccio and of his crucifixion on La Verna were with him now. It was a matter of goading himself to further effort by the first scene and of jealously treasuring the last scene:

"With the Lord born for us, it has become a matter of propriety for us to save ourselves."—MP 114.

"I have hidden Your words in my heart, that I might not sin against you."—1C 96.

That, and the happiness of seeing fulfilled one of the holiest wishes ever uttered:

"O Lord Jesus Christ, I entreat you to give me two graces before I die:" . . . (see no. **19**).

263. He seemed never to get his fill of suffering. When the brother waiting on him suggested that he ask God for alleviation, he turned on him in the half bantering half earnest way he could assume:

"Brother, did I not know that it is sheer

simplicity in you, I should henceforth loathe your company for venturing to consider the judgments of God on my behalf blame-worthy."

Reduced as he was, he went on his knees:

"I give you thanks, O Lord God, for these pains of mine, and I beg you, my Lord, add a hundredfold to them if it please you. It will be most agreeable to me that in afflicting me with pain you do not spare me. Fulfilling your holy will is more than ample comfort to me."—B 14.

264. He had a holy indifference as to the particular kind of pain—his pain or martyrdom:

"My son, that ever has been and remains more dear, lovable and acceptable to me which it pleases the Lord my God to have happen to me or concerning me, and I desire always in everything to be found altogether in harmony and compliance with his will alone. But as for exchanging with any kind of martyrdom, to bear this illness for even three days would be more distressful; and I am not saying this in estimation of the re-ward but only of the distress the suffering causes."—1 C 107.

265. At that he feared he might be too indul-gent to his body:

"What do you think, my son, about my

conscience often murmuring over the care I give my body? It is afraid I am too indulgent toward it in its ailment and that I am trying to relieve it with choice blandishments. Not that it can take anything with pleasure anymore, now that it is worn out by long infirmity and all the relish of taste has gone from it."—2C 210.

266. But he was fair to Brother Ass, as he often called his body:

"I bear it witness, my son, that it has been obedient in everything, that it has spared itself in no particular but fairly rushed headlong at every command. It shirked no exertion, evaded no inconvenience, so long as it could accomplish what was ordered. On this point I and it have agreed perfectly that we would serve Christ the Lord without any reluctance.

"Be glad, brother body, and forgive me, for see, I am glad to do your pleasure now. I gladly hurry to meet your plaintive emotions."—2C 211.

267. Francis did ask for certain gratifications. At Rieti, when the pain was great, strangely his olden youth days seemed to come back to him. Or was it thinking ahead to heavenly harmonies?

"The children of this world have no understanding for the sacred designs of God. Thus, musical instruments, once destined to serve

the Divine praises, have been converted by
human passion into a debauch for the ears.
So, brother, I wish you would quietly borrow
a lute and bring it here in order to give some
measure of comfort to pain-filled brother
body by playing a decent tune!"

But the brother reminded him of possible
scandal:

"Let us do without it then, brother. It is
good to give up many a thing for fear of
offending other people's sensibilities."

But the next morning:

"The Lord, who comforts the afflicted, has
never left me without consolation. For look,
after having no chance to listen to mortal
lute play, I have listened to a sweeter lute."
—2C 126.

268. At Assisi too, he had the brothers often
sing The Praises (**36**) during the day. Brother
Elias, so says the *Mirror*, reminded him that
most likely people rather expected him to be
thinking of death. Francis reminded Elias of a
vision Elias had once recounted to Francis, to the
effect that Francis would die in two years:

"Before you had that vision, by the grace
of God, who suggests all that is good to the
heart and puts it on the lips of his faithful, I
often gave thought night and day to my
death. But from that hour on when you saw

the vision, I have been more concerned than ever to think daily of my dying day.

"So, brother, do let me go on being happy in the Lord and his praises amid my infirmities, for, the grace of the Holy Ghost helping, I am so far in union and unison with my Lord that I can now through his mercy well be jolly in him, the Most High."—MP 121.

269. He was thinking of death. He left a brief last will in three sentences while at Assisi in April 1226, sometimes called the little Testament:

"Since due to my weakness and the pains of my ailment I am unable to speak, I make known my will briefly to all my brothers present and future in these three words:

"That in token of their remembering me and of my blessing and last will they do always love and give respect to one another;

"That they do always love and give respect to our holy Lady Poverty; and

"That they do always remain loyal and submissive to the prelates and all the clergy of the holy Roman Church."—MP 88.

270. On the way out to St. Mary's from Assisi he asked his carriers to turn him once again, for the last time, toward Assisi—see it he could not, but he could bless it:

"Be blest of God, O holy city! On your account many souls shall be saved, many servants of God shall dwell in you, and from your midst many shall be chosen for the kingdom of life everlasting."—LF 4th Stigm.

The *Mirror* relates a longer blessing:

"O Lord, just as of old this city was, I believe, the home and abode of wicked people, so I see that through your abundant mercy, as the time pleased you, you have given singular proof in it of your plentiful mercies. It is purely of your goodness that you have chosen it for yourself as the home and abode of those who were to know you truly and give glory to your holy name, manifesting to all Christendom the odor of good fame, a holy life, the truest doctrine, and Gospel perfection.

"I beseech you then, O Lord Jesus Christ, Father of mercies, disregard our ingratitude and keep mindful ever of the most abundant fatherly love you have displayed in it, that it may ever be the home and abode of such as truly acknowledge you and glorify your blest and most glorious name for ever and ever. Amen."—MP 124.

271. The farewell to Assisi was one of a series of leave-takings. For as such we may well consider, first, his summons to all creation, from Master Sun down, to give praise to God. The *Mirror* repeats that he called these praises *The Canticle of Brother Sun* (MP 101 and 119).

The Canticle of Brother Sun was begun at Assisi in the summer of 1225. It grew out of Francis's joy in suffering and the plaint that man uses God's creatures to offend him with them:

"If the emperor were to give a subject of his an entire kingdom, would the subject not have cause to be very glad? But if he gave him all the empire, would he not be much happier still?

"Then I too should be very glad at my ailments and trials and take comfort in the Lord, always giving thanks to God the Father, his only Son our Lord Jesus Christ, and the Holy Ghost for the great grace done me by the Lord in deigning to assure me while still living in the flesh, of his kingdom.

"For his praise, therefore, and for our consolation and the edification of our neighbor I want to compose a new hymn about the Lord's creatures, of which we make daily use, without which we cannot live, and with which the human race greatly offends its Creator. And we go on being ungrateful for a grace and benefit so great, not praising the Lord Creator and Giver of all good things as we ought."

He meditated awhile, then intoned the Canticle through the stanza on Sister Earth, telling his brothers to sing it thereafter to the people, saying when they did so:

"We are the minstrels of the Lord, and for

what we offer we want to be requited by you to the extent that you persevere in true repentance. For what else are the servants of God but his minstrels, whose work it is to lift up people's hearts and move them to spiritual gladness?"—MP 100.

A few months before his death a year later, again at Assisi, when a feud broke out between the bishop and the mayor, he said:

"It is a great shame for us servants of God that the bishop and the mayor antagonize each other so, and nobody is intervening for peace between them."

So saying, he added the stanza on peace and pardon to the Canticle of Brother Sun. Then he sent brothers to bid the mayor to the bishop's, saying:

"Go, and in the presence of bishop and mayor and the rest in their company sing the Canticle of Brother Sun. I trust to the Lord that he will soon humble their hearts and they will go back to their former love and friendship."—MP 101.

The last stanza, on Brother Death, came when he was assured he would die quite soon. He bade Brothers Angelo and Leo to sing the Canticle with the added stanza.—MP 123.

The complete text is given below in (**281**).

272. We have seen how considerate St. Francis was in taking leave of the Ladies of St. Clare

(**119-122**) and of the Lady Giacoma of Settesoli
(**116-118**). There was the farewell to Brother
Bernard:

"Where is my first-born? May God, the
Father of our Lord Jesus Christ, bless you
with every spiritual and heavenly blessing in
Christ. You were the first to be chosen in this
holy order to give the example of following
Jesus Christ in Gospel poverty. Not only did
you for the love of Christ, give up and distribute to the poor wholly and freely everything you possessed, but you likewise made
of yourself a sacrifice of sweetness to God in
this order.

"Then blest shall you be by our Lord Jesus
Christ, and by me his poor little servant, with
eternal blessings, wherever you go and stay,
and wake and sleep, and live and die. He who
blesses you shall be filled with blessings, he
who speaks ill of you shall not be without his
punishment."—LF 6.

273. There was Minister General Elias:

"I bless you, my son, in all and through
all things. And as the Most High has increased my brothers and sons in your hands,
so do I bless them all on you and in you. May
God, the King of all things, bless you in
Heaven and on earth. I bless you as much as
I can and more than I can, and what I have

not the power to do, may He be able to do in you who can do all things.

"God be mindful of your work and your endeavors and may your portion be reserved where the just are requited. May you find every blessing you desire, and may whatever you ask for worthily, be fulfilled."—1C 108.

274. There followed his leave of the brothers at Assisi:

"Farewell, my sons all, in the fear of God, and abide in it always. For great trial is coming upon you and tribulation is drawing near. Happy they who will persevere in what they have begun, for scandals to come will separate some from that course. I am hastening on to the Lord, even now I trust I am going on to my God, whom I have served in devotion of spirit."—1C 108.

275. There were a few parting words with his physicians, as with the one who bade him desist from his constant weeping to spare his eyesight:

"Oh, brother physician, we should not for the love of the light we possess in common with the flies repulse, even in the least, being visited by the eternal light. The spirit has not received the blessing of light for the sake of the body; the body has received it for the sake of the spirit."—B 5.

276. "Brother physician, tell me without

misgiving whether death is very near; it will be the gate of life to me."—2C 217.

Or, as the first Book of Conformities 12 has it:

"Tell me plainly, I say, and do not fear. For by the grace of God I am not a timid little heart, that I should fear death. The grace of the Holy Ghost helping, I am so at one with my Lord that I will not be sad over dying, nor rejoice any more over living longer. I will be equally pleased at life or death."

277. A few final directions were given at St. Mary's:

"I have done my duty. Christ teach you yours."—2C 214.

"I wish to have no care about eating or drinking, brother. I put it all into your hands: if you give me anything, I will take it; if not, I will not ask for it."—MP 107.

"When you see that I am being brought toward the end, lay me naked on the floor as you found me three days ago, and let me lie there in death for as long a time as it takes to walk a mile leisurely."—2C 217.

Here belong also his words about treasuring St. Mary of the Angels (**66**).

278. His last words of farewell to the brothers, cited later by Elias in his notification to all the brothers, were:

"See, my son, I am being called by God. I

forgive my brothers, the absent as well as the present, all their offenses and failings, and absolve them as far as I can. Tell them about this and bless them all for me."—1C 109.

279. All-embracing was his
"Welcome, Brother Death!"—2C 217.

280. Psalm 141, said by him "as well as he could," was among the very last things he uttered (1C 109):

"I cried to the Lord with my voice, with my voice I made supplication to the Lord.
In his sight I pour out my prayer, and before him I declare my trouble.
When my spirit failed me, then you knew my paths.
In this way where I walked, they have hidden a snare for me.
I looked on my right hand and beheld, and there was no one that would know me.
Flight hath failed me, and there is no one that has regard for my soul.
I cried to you, O Lord; I said, You are my hope, my portion in the land of the living.
Attend to my supplication, for I am brought very low.
Deliver me from my persecutors, for they are stronger than I.

Bring my soul out of prison that I may praise your name, the just wait for me until you reward me."

281. Thus died the Little Poor Man of Assisi, the Seraph aglow with the love of God and love of everything else only in God and for God. His life is well summarized in his immortal *Canticle of Brother Sun*, of which God is the absorbing subject, marshaling all his creature chorus led by God's earthly image Brother Sun to sound his praises*. A counterpart on earth of Heaven's eternal hymnody is

THE CANTICLE OF BROTHER SUN

Most high, almighty, and good Lord,
Yours is the praise, the glory, honor,
    blessing all.
To you, Most High, alone of right they do
    belong,
And no mortal man is fit to mention you.

Be praised, my Lord, of all your creature
    world,
And first of all Sir Brother Sun,
Who brings the day, and light you give to
    us through him,
And beautiful is he, agleam with mighty
    splendor:
Of you, Most High, he gives us indication.

Be praised, my Lord, through Sisters
    Moon and Stars:
In the heavens you have formed them,
    bright and fair and precious.

Be praised, my Lord, through Brother Wind,
Through Air, and cloudy, clear, and every
  kind of Weather,
By whom you give your creatures
  sustenance.

Be praised, my Lord, through Sister Water,
For greatly useful, lowly, precious, chaste
  is she.

Be praised, my Lord, through Brother Fire,
Through whom you brighten up the night,
And fair he is, and gay, and vigorous, and
  strong.

Be praised, O Lord, through our sister
  Mother Earth,

For she sustains and guides our life,

And yields us divers fruits, with tinted
  flowers, and grass.

Be praised, my Lord, through those who
  pardon give for love of you,

And bear infirmity and tribulation:

Blessed they who suffer it in peace,
For of you, Most High, they shall be
  crowned.

Be praised, my Lord, through our Brother
  Death of Body,

From whom no man among the living can
  escape.

Woe to those who in mortal sins will die;
Blessed those whom he will find in your
  most holy graces,
For the second death will do no harm to
  them.

Praise and bless my Lord, and thank him
  too,
And serve him all, in great humility.

Part XII

Saint Francis
Leaves a Legacy

PART XII

St. Francis leaves a legacy

St. Francis lives on in the three orders he has founded—the Friars Minor, the Poor Clares, and the Third Order—and in the untold host of his admirers of every faith and no faith in every walk of life.

282. Treasured, however, as a kind of summary of the spiritual widsom embodied in the three orders, with its deep faith, its reverence for Church and clergy, its insistence on poverty in a spiritual as well as a material sense—is the

TESTAMENT OF ST. FRANCIS

The Lord gave me, Brother Francis, the grace of beginning to do penance in this way: that, when I was in sins, it seemed extremely bitter to me to look at lepers, and the Lord himself led me in among them and I practiced mercy with them. And when I came away from them, what seemed bitter to me, was changed to sweetness of spirit and body for me. And after that I did not wait long and left the world. And the Lord gave me so much faith in churches that I prayed and said simply thus: "We adore you, O Lord

Jesus Christ, here and at all your churches all over the world, and we bless you, because by your holy cross you have redeemed the world."*

282a. After that the Lord gave and gives me so much faith in priests that live subject to the law of the holy Roman Church, by reason of their Orders, that even if they were to persecute me I will take recourse to them. And if I had as much wisdom as Solomon had, and were to come upon poorly-off priests out in the world, it is my will not to preach against their pleasure in parishes where they are stationed. And it is my will to love and honor them and all others as my masters; and I will not regard sin in them, because I discern the Son of God in them and they are my masters. And I do this for the reason that in this world I see nothing bodily of the most high Son of God himself but his most holy Body and Blood, which they have in charge and they alone administer to others.

282b. And I want these most holy mysteries above all else to be honored and venerated and kept in choice places. Wherever I find his most holy names and written words in improper places, I mean to pick them up and I beg that they be picked up and put in a respectable place. And all the theologians and persons who administer the most holy words of God, we must honor and respect as people who minister spirit and life to us.

282c. And after the Lord gave me some brothers, there was nobody to show me what to do; but the Most High himself revealed to me that I was to live according to the form of the Holy Gospel. And I caused it to be written down simply and in a few words, and the Lord Pope approved it for me. And those who came to take up this life, gave all they could possess to the poor, and they were content with one tunic patched inside and out if they wished, besides a cincture and drawers. And we wished to have nothing else.

282d. We who were clerics said the Office like other clerics, the lay members said the Our Father, and we were quite happy spending the time in churches. And we were plain people and at everybody's service. And I worked with my hands, and I wish to work; and I wish earnestly to have all the rest of the brothers work at employment such as conforms with propriety. Those who know none, should learn, not from the desire to get the price of the labor, but for example's sake and to repel idleness. And should the wages of our work not be given to us, let us take recourse to the table of the Lord by seeking alms from door to door.

282e. The Lord revealed to me that we should speak this greeting: The Lord give you peace. Let the brothers be on their guard against accepting in any way the churches, the lowly dwellings, and anything else constructed for them unless they are as is becoming to the holy poverty which we have promised in the rule; always putting up in them like strangers and pilgrims.

282f. I firmly command all the brothers in obedience that wherever they are they do not dare, either personally or through an interposed person, seek any letter at the Roman Curia, neither for a church or any other place, nor on pretext of their preaching or of persecution directed against their person; but, wherever they are not welcome, let them flee to some other land to do penance there with God's blessing. And I wish firmly to obey the minister general of this brotherhood and whatever other guardian he may be pleased to give me. And I wish to be so much a captive in his hands that I cannot go about or do anything against his orders and his will, for he is my master. And however plain and weak I am, yet I wish always to have a cleric to do the Office with me as is contained in the rule.

232g. And let the rest of the brothers all be bound to obey their guardians and perform the Office according to the rule. And should any be found who might not be performing the Office according to the rule, or might want to deviate any other way, or might not be Catholic, let all the brothers, wherever they are, be bound in obedience wherever they may find anyone of the kind to present him to the custos nearest to the place where they have found him. And let the custos be bound firmly in obedience to guard that person strongly day and night like a man in chains, so that he cannot be snatched from his hands till he in person shall place him in the hands of his minister. And let the minister be bound firmly in obedience to send him by such brothers as shall guard him day and night like a man in chains till they present him before the Lord of Ostia, who is the master, protector and corrector of all the brotherhood.

282h. And let not the brothers say, This is a different rule! For, this is a reminder, a warning, an exhortation and my testament, which I, poor little Brother Francis, make to you, my blest brothers, to the end that we may observe the rule we have promised the Lord, in a better Catholic way. And let the minister general and all the other ministers and custodes be bound in obedience not to add to these words nor to take from them. And besides the rule let them always have this writing about them. And at all the chapters they hold, let them when they read the rule, read these words too. And I strictly command all my brothers both clerical and lay, in obedience, not to put glosses on the rule or on these words, saying, They are to be understood thus: but, just as the Lord has given it to me to speak and write the rule and these words simply and purely, thus simply and purely are you to understand them and with holy practice to observe them to the last.

282i. And whoever shall observe these things, may he in Heaven be filled with the blessing of the most high Father and on earth be filled with the blessing of his beloved Son together with the most holy Spirit the Paraclete, and all the powers of the Heavens and all the saints. And I, Brother Francis, your poor little one and servant, as much as ever I can, confirm for you, within and without, this most holy blessing. Amen.

283. Full of the unction of the Holy Spirit, with its frequent Scriptural passages, the prayer incorporated in it, and its wise, detailed directions is the so-called

FIRST RULE OF THE FRIARS MINOR

This Rule was submitted by St. Francis for the approval of Pope Innocent III soon after founding the order. Pope Innocent approved it orally April 23, 1209. About fourteen years later a more concise and pointed rule was found necessary to meet the needs of the growing order. Then St. Francis submitted the Second Rule, the rule now in force, for approval. Pope Honorius III approved it in a formal document dated November 29, 1223, the day now observed as All Saints day of the order.

The First Rule in the wording usually published comprises additions made to the very first text in the course of the fourteen years it was observed; additions made to stress certain points, or to set down in words what at first seemed self-evident; additions such as, for example, that in **283d,** "to roam abroad beyond obedience," from a bull of Pope Honorius III Sept. 22, 1220.

There is no substantial difference between the First and the Second Rule. Pope Honorius himself calls the Second Rule the rule approved by Pope Innocent. Nevertheless, the First Rule has always been treasured in the order as a fuller expression of the sentiments of St. Francis and as an embodiment of the spirit common to all the three orders of St. Francis—Friars, Poor Clares, and Tertiaries. The text is as follows, Scriptural references inserted:

283a. In the name of the Father and of the Son and of the Holy Ghost. Amen.

Let Brother Francis and whoever will be the head of this order promise obedience and reverence to the Lord Pope Innocent and his successors. And the rest of the brothers are bound to obey Brother Francis and his successors.

1. *The brothers are to live in obedience, without property, and in chastity*

283b. The rule and life of these brothers is this, that they live in obedience, in chastity, and without property, and follow the teaching and the footsteps of our Lord Jesus Christ, who says: "If you wish to be perfect, go and sell everything you have and give it to the poor, and you shall have treasure in Heaven, and come, follow me" (Mt. 19, 21); and, "If anybody wishes to come after me, let him deny himself and carry his cross and follow me" (Mt. 16, 24); likewise, "If anybody wishes to come to me and he does not hate his father and mother and wife and children and brothers and sisters, yes his very life, he cannot be my disciple" (Lk. 14, 26); "And everyone who leaves father or mother, or brothers or sisters, or wife or children, or houses or fields for my sake, shall receive a hundredfold and possess eternal life" (Mt. 19, 29).

2. *The reception of the brothers, and their clothing*

283c. If anybody, desiring at God's inspiration to take up this life, comes to our brothers, let him be kindly received by them.

And if he is resolved to take up our life, the brothers must be very careful not to meddle with his temporal affairs but should present him to their minister as soon as they can. The minister, however, should welcome him kindly and encourage him, and take pains to explain the way of our life to him. That done, if the aforesaid is willing and able to do so in the right spirit and without hindrance, let him sell whatever he owns and make the effort to distribute it all to the poor. But the brothers and the ministers of the brothers should beware not to meddle in his affairs in any way, and not to accept any money either personally or through any intermediary; if, however, they are in need, they may accept the necessaries of the body other than money to meet their need, like other poor people.

283d. And when the person comes back, the minister should grant him the probation clothes for a year, that is, two tunics without a cowl, and a cincture, and drawers, and a chaperon reaching to the cincture. When, however, the year and term of probation are over, he should be received to obedience. After that it will not be lawful for him to pass over to any other order or "to roam abroad beyond obedience," according to the orders of the Lord Pope. For, according to the Gospel, nobody putting his hand to the plow and looking backward is fit for the kingdom of God (Lk. 9, 62).

But should anybody come that cannot give away his goods without hindrance though he is spiritually minded to do so, let him give them up and that suffices for him. Nobody is to be received contrary to the manner and form of Holy Church.

283e. But the rest of the brothers, who have promised obedience, shall have one tunic with a cowl, and another without a cowl if necessary, and a cincture and drawers. And all the brothers shall dress in clothes of low value, and they may patch them with sacking and other pieces with the blessing of God; for the Lord says in the Gospel, they that live in costly dress and in luxury and are dressed in soft garments, are in the houses of kings (cf. Mt. 11, 8 and Lk. 7, 25). And though they be called hypocrites, let them not quit their good life, nor let them look for expensive clothes in this world, so that they can have their robe in the kingdom of Heaven.

3. *The Divine Office and fasting*

283f. The Lord says: This kind of demons cannot get out except through fasting and prayer (cf. Mk. 9, 28), and again: When you fast, do not grow sad like hypocrites (Mt. 6, 16).

For that reason all the brothers, whether clerical or lay, should perform the Divine Office with the praises and prayers as is prescribed for them. The clerics shall perform the Office and say it for the living and the dead according to the custom for the clergy; but in amends for any shortcoming and negligence of the brothers let them say the Miserere mei Deus with the Pater noster every day, and the De profundis with the Pater noster for the dead. And they may have only the books needed to discharge their Office. And also the lay brothers who know how to read may have a psalter, but those who do not know how to read, are not to have a book.

But the lay brothers shall say the Creed and twenty-four Pater nosters with the Gloria Patri for the Matins, for the Lauds five, for the Prime the Creed and seven Pater nosters with the Gloria Patri, for each the Tierce, the Sext, and the None seven, for the Vespers twelve, and for the Compline the Creed and seven Pater nosters with the Gloria Patri; for the deceased seven Pater nosters with the Requiem aeternam and for the shortcoming and negligence of the brothers daily three Pater nosters.

283g. And likewise all the brothers should fast from the feast of All Saints till the

Nativity of our Lord, and from Epiphany, when our Lord Jesus Christ began to fast, till Easter; at other times, however, according to this rule of life, they should not be bound to fast except on Friday. And, according to the Gospel, they are free to eat of whatever foods are put before them (cf. Lk. 10, 8).

4. *The ministers and the rest of the brothers in their mutual relation*

283h. In the name of the Lord, any brothers who are made ministers and servants of the rest of the brothers, shall station their brothers in the provinces and places where they may be, and they shall often visit them and direct and encourage them spiritually. And all my other blest brothers shall be careful to obey them in matters that concern the welfare of their soul and are not contrary to our way of life.

And they shall act toward one another as our Lord says: "Whatever you wish people to do to you, do in turn to them" (Mt. 7, 12); and, "What you do not want done to you, do not do to anyone else" (Tob. 4, 16).

And let the ministers and servants recall that the Lord says, "I have not come to be ministered to, but to minister" (Mt. 20, 28); and that to them has been committed the care of the brothers' souls, of whom, if any- one should be lost through their fault and bad example, they shall have to give an account before our Lord Jesus Christ on the day of judgment.

5. *Correction of brothers at fault*

283i. Therefore, watch over your souls and those of your brothers, because "it is terrible to fall into the hands of the living God" (Hebr. 10, 31). If, however, anyone of the ministers commands any brother to do anything against our way of life or against his conscience, the brother should not be held to obey him, for that is not obedience if a fault or sin is committed by it.

Nevertheless let all the brothers who are subject to the ministers and servants, sensibly and carefully observe what is done by the ministers and servants. And if they see that anyone of them is living carnally rather than in the right spirit of our way of life, if he does not amend after a threefold warning, he should be reported to the minister and servant of the entire brotherhood at the Pentecost chapter, regardless of any opposition.

283j. If, on the other hand, there is anyone among the brothers, wherever they be, who is minded to live carnally rather than spiritually, the brothers with whom he lives, should admonish, instruct and correct him with humility and care. But if after a threefold caution he has no will to amend, they should as soon as they can send him or send word to his minister and servant, and that minister and servant shall do with him as under God will seem the most advisable.

And all the brothers, ministers and servants as well as the rest, should take care not to be disturbed or angered over anyone else's sin or bad example, because the Devil likes to worsen many over one person's sin; but let them spirtually, as well as they can, help the one who has sinned, for it is not the well who need the physician but the sick (Mt. 9, 12).

283k. Likewise, let the brothers all not aspire to any power and authority, above all among themselves. For the Lord says in the Gospel, "the rulers of the Gentiles lord it over them, and their great men exercise authority over them" (Mt. 20, 25). It should not be thus among the brothers, but who-ever wishes to be the greater among them, should be their minister and servant (cf. Mt. 20, 26), and he who is the elder among them, should be like the younger (cf. Lk. 22, 26).

And no brother should do or say anything evil to any other. On the contrary, they should rather be willing to serve and obey one another in the charity of their spirit. And such is the true and holy obedience of our Lord Jesus Christ.

And let all the brothers at any time they have turned from the commandments of God and wandered outside the bounds of obedience, understand that, as the prophet says (cf. Ps. 118, 21), they are under a curse outside of obedience for as long as they knowingly remain in such a sin. And when they persevere in the Lord's commandments, to which they have pledged themselves in the holy Gospel and their way of life, let them understand that they abide in true obedience and are blest by the Lord.

6. Recourse of the brothers to the ministers, and no brother to be called prior

283L. If the brothers, at whatever stations they are, cannot observe our way of life, they should have recourse to their minister as soon as they can, indicating that to him. The minister in turn should endeavor to provide for them in the way he would want it done for him if he were in a similar situation.

And no one should be called prior, but let all in general be called lesser brothers. And each should wash the other's feet.

7. Manner of serving and working

283m. The brothers all, at whatever stations they may be among other people for service and work, are not to be personal attendants, nor secretaries, nor managers in households where they are in service; nor are they to accept any position that may cause scandal or bring harm on their soul (Mk. 8, 36); but let them be of the lesser stations and subject to everybody in that household.

And the brothers that know any craft, should go to work and practice what craft they may know as long as it is not contrary to the good of their soul and they can ply it with propriety. For the prophet says: "Because you shall eat the labors of your hands, you are blessed, and it will be well with you" (Ps. 127, 2); and the apostle: "Whoever does not want to work, shall not eat" (2 Thes. 3, 10); and, in whatever craft or employment anybody is called, let him remain there (1 Cor. 7, 24). And for their work they may accept everything necessary except money. And should it be necessary, they can go out for alms like the rest of the brothers. And they may have the tools and instruments needed for their crafts.

All the brothers should endeavor to keep hard at good occupation, because it is written: "Always be doing some good work, so that the Devil may find you busy" (St. Jerome, Ep. 125), and again: "Idleness is the enemy of the soul" (St. Anselm, Ep. 49). Thus servants of God ought always to keep at prayer or some other good occupation.

Let the brothers wherever they may be, in hermitages or other places, take heed not to make any place their own and maintain it against anybody else. And let whoever may approach them, whether friend or foe, or thief or robber, be received kindly. And wherever the brothers are and in whatever situation they may find themselves, they should be careful to show the right spirit of reverence and honor toward one another, without murmuring (1 Peter 4, 9). And let the brothers take heed not to appear sad exteriorly and be gloomy hypocrites, but let them prove to be joyful in the Lord, and merry and becomingly courteous.

8. *The brothers are not to accept money*

283n. The Lord commands in the Gospel: Look to it, beware of all ill-will and avarice, and keep yourselves from all the concerns of this world and the cares of this life (cf. Lk. 12, 15; 21, 34). For that reason none of the brothers, wherever he may be or wherever he goes, shall in any way take along money or coin, or accept it, or cause it to be accepted; neither for the purpose of clothing or books, nor as payment for any work done, nor in short for any reason, except for the evident need of sick brothers; because we ought to have no greater use and regard for money and coin than for stones. And the Devil is set to blind those who crave it or value it more than stones.

Let us, therefore, who have given up everything, take heed lest for anything so paltry we may lose the kingdom of Heaven. And should we find coins anywhere, let us not bother about them any more than the dust we tread under foot, for it is vanity of vanities, and all vanity (Eccles. 1, 2). And if ever, which God forbid, it should happen that any brother collects or has money or coin, except only because of the aforesaid need of the sick, all the brothers should regard him as a false brother, and a thief and robber and purse-keeper, unless he repents sincerely.

And in no way are the brothers to accept money as alms or have it accepted, or to solicit it or have it solicited, or coin for any of the houses or places; and they are not to go out with a person soliciting money or coin for such places. Other services, however, that are not contrary to our way of life, the brothers may perform with God's blessing.

Still, when there is evident need on the part of the lepers, the brothers shall be allowed to seek alms for them. But they should beware very much of money. Likewise the brothers all shall beware of going about from place to place in quest of any filthy lucre.

9. *Soliciting alms*

2830. All the brothers should try to follow the humility and poverty of our Lord Jesus Christ, and should mind that we ought not have anything else of all this world except that, as the apostle says, "having food and clothing enough, we be content with these" (1 Tim. 6, 8). And they should be glad at associating with people of low rank and estimation, the poor and the feeble, the sick and the lepers, and people begging at the wayside.

And should it be necessary, let them go out for alms. And they should not be ashamed of it, but mind rather that our Lord Jesus Christ, the Son of the almighty living God, "set his face like a very hard rock" (Is. 50, 7), and was not ashamed and was poor and shelterless and lived on alms—both he and the blessed Virgin and his disciples. And were people to embarrass them and not want to give them any alms, they should thank God for it, because in return for the embarrassment they will receive great honor at the judgment seat of our Lord Jesus Christ. And they should know that the embarrassment is charged not against those who suffer it but against those who inflict it.

And alms are a heritage and just claim due

to the poor, which our Lord Jesus Christ acquired for us. And the brothers who have the labor of obtaining them, will have a great reward, and will help the donors gain and acquire it, because everything people leave behind them in the world, is lost to them, but they will have a return from the Lord for the charity and the alms-deeds they have done.

283p. And each should with assurance make known his need to the other, so he can find and supply what is necessary to him. And every one of them should love and take care of his brother like a mother loves and takes care of her son, to whatever extent God will give them the grace. And "let the one who eats not despise the one who does not eat, and let the one who does not eat, not judge the one who eats" (Rom. 14, 3).

And whenever the necessity arises, it shall be allowed for all the brothers wherever they may be to make use of whatever kind of food the people can eat, as the Lord tells of David, who "ate the loaves of proposition, which it was not lawful except for the priests to eat" (Mk. 2, 26). And they should mind that the Lord says: "But take heed to yourselves lest your hearts be overburdened with surfeiting and drunkenness and the cares of his life, and that day come upon you suddenly; for like a snare it will come on all who dwell on the face of the earth" (Lk. 21, 34-5).

In like manner in a time of manifest need let all the brothers act with regard to what they need the way the Lord gives them the grace, for necessity has no law.

10. *The sick brothers*

283q. Should any brother fall into sickness, wherever he be the rest of the brothers are not to leave him without one of the brothers, or several if necessary, being appointed to wait on him as they would want to be waited on. But in very great urgency they can leave him to some other person who shall have to do what his illness requires.

And I ask the sick brother to thank the Creator for it all, and well or sick he should want to be just as our Lord wants him to be, since God rears all whom he has destined for eternal life with the goad of affliction and infirmity and with the spirit of compunction, as the Lord says: "Those whom I love, I rebuke and chastise" (Apoc. 3, 19). If, however, he grows disturbed or angry either with God or with his brothers, or perhaps impatiently demands remedies from too great a desire to relieve the flesh, which soon will die and is an enemy of the soul, that is a result of the evil in him and he is carnal, and he does not act like one of the brothers, because he loves his body more than his soul.

11. *No malicious talk or detraction among the brothers, but only mutual love*

234r. The brothers all shall be on their guard against slandering anybody, or getting into disputes (2 Tim. 2, 14); sooner let them keep altogether silent so far as God gives them the grace. Nor let them quarrel among themselves, nor with others, but keep minded to make a humble reply, saying to themselves, "We are unprofitable servants" (Lk. 17, 10). And they must not bear anger, for "everyone who is angry with his brother shall be liable to judgment; and whoever says to his brother, Raca, shall be liable to the Council; and whoever says, You fool, shall be liable to the fire of Hell" (Mt. 5, 22).

And they should love one another, as the Lord says, "This is my commandment that you love one another as I have loved you" (Jn. 15, 12). And they must show by their actions what love they bear one another (cf. Jas. 2, 18), as the apostle says: "Let us love not in word or speech, but in deed and truth" (1 Jn. 3, 18). And let them not speak untruthfully about anyone (Tit. 3, 2), nor bear tales, nor spread evil about others, for it is written, "Whisperers and detractors are people hateful to God" (Rom. 1, 29).

And let them be "restrained, exercising all gentleness toward all people" (Tit. 3, 2).

They should not sit in judgment on others, nor condemn them, and, as the Lord says, they should not give attention to the tiny sins of others (cf. Mt. 7, 3) but rather count over their own in the bitterness of their soul (cf. Is. 38, 15).

And they should make the effort to enter in at the narrow gate (Lk. 13, 24), because the Lord says the gate and road leading to life is small and narrow, and few there are who find it (Mt. 7, 14).

12. *Avoiding evil looks and association with women*

283s. The brothers all, wherever they are or go, shall be on their guard against evil looks and association with women, and none shall confer alone with them. Let the priests speak respectfully with them in administering Penance or any spiritual advice. And let no woman whatever be taken under his obedience by any brother, but once the spiritual direction has been given her, let her live her life of penance where she chooses.

And let us all keep ourselves and all our faculties very clean, since the Lord says, "Anybody who looks at a woman with desire for her, has already committed adultery with her in his heart" (Mt. 5, 28).

13. *The punishment of fornicators*

283t. Should anyone of the brothers at the Devil's impulse commit fornication, he shall have taken from him the habit of the order, which he has forfeited by his shameful depravity; he shall lay it aside altogether and be expelled entirely from our order. And thereafter let him do penance for his sins.

14. *How the brothers should act in the world*

283u. As the brothers go about in the world, they should take nothing with them on the way, neither bag, nor purse, nor bread, nor money, nor staff; and whenever they enter a house, they should first say, Peace to this house. And while they remain at that house, they should eat and drink what the people there have (cf. Lk. 9, 3 and 10, 4-8).

They should not resent evil (Mt. 5, 39). Rather, if anybody hits them on one cheek, let them offer him the other, and if anyone takes away their outer dress, let them not refuse their tunic either. Let them give to everybody who asks, and if anyone takes away what belongs to them, let them not demand it back (Lk. 6, 29-30).

15. *The brothers not to keep any animal, nor to ride horseback*

283v. I enjoin on all my brothers both clerical and lay, as they go about in the world

or stay at any place, not at all to have any
kind of animal, neither about them, nor in
anyone else's care, nor in any other way. Nor
are they permitted to ride horseback unless
compelled to by infirmity or great need.

16. *Those going among the Saracens and other
    infidels*

283w. The Lord says: "Look, I am sending
you among wolves like sheep. You are therefore to be as wise as serpents and as simple as
doves" (Mt. 10, 16). For that reason whoever
of the brothers wish on Divine inspiration to
go among the Saracens and other infidels,
may go there with the permission of their
minister and servant. Their minister, however, should give them the permission and
not oppose them, if he sees they are fit to be
sent; for he shall have to give an account of it
to the Lord if he acts inadvisedly in this and
like matters.

The brothers who go, however, may conduct themselves among them spiritually in
two ways. One way is not to start strife and
contention, but "be subject to every human
creature for God's sake" (1 Pet. 2, 13) and so
profess themselves to be Christians. The other
way is that when they see it pleases God, they
proclaim the word of God, to have them believe in almighty God, Father, Son, and Holy
Ghost, the Creator of all things, and in the

Son, the Redeemer and Savior, and have them be baptized and become Christians, since "unless a person be born again of the water and the Holy Ghost, he cannot enter into the kingdom of God" (Jn. 3, 5).

These and other things as may please God they may tell them and others, for the Lord says in the Gospel, "Everyone who confesses me before men, I too will confess him before my Father, who is in Heaven" (Mt. 10, 32); and, "Whoever will be ashamed of me and my words, the Son of Man will be ashamed of him when he comes in his majesty and that of the Father and of the holy angels" (Lk. 9, 26).

283x. And all the brothers, wherever they are, should call to mind that they have surrendered themselves and relinquished their person to our Lord Jesus Christ, and so they must for love of him face his enemies both visible and invisible, for the Lord says: "Whoever loses his life for my sake, will save it" (Mk. 8, 35; Lk. 9, 24) for life everlasting. "Blessed are those who suffer persecution for justice's sake, for theirs is the kingdom of Heaven" (Mt. 5, 10). "If they have persecuted me, they will persecute you" (Jn. 15, 20). "If they persecute you in one city, flee to another one" (Mt. 10, 23).

Blessed are you when people hate you and speak evil of you: and when they single you

out and revile you and strike out your name
as something evil, and when lyingly they
utter everything evil against you on my
account: rejoice on that day and be glad, because your reward is great in Heaven (cf.
Mt. 5, 11-12; Lk. 6, 22-23).

"But I say to you as my friends, do not
be terrified by them, and do not fear those
who kill the body and then have nothing
more that they can do" (cf. Mt. 10, 28; Lk.
12, 4). "See to it that you are not disturbed"
(Mt. 24, 6). For "by your patience, you will
assure your souls" (Lk. 21, 19). "Whatsoever
perseveres to the end, will be saved" (Mt.
10, 22).

17. *Preachers*

283y. None of the brothers shall preach
contrary to the procedure and doctrine of the
holy Roman Church, and unless the license
has been granted him by his minister. The
minister in turn shall be on his guard not to
grant any the license inadvisedly. All the
brothers, however, shall preach by their
actions.

And let no minister or preacher seize on
the ministry of the brothers or the office of
preaching as his right, but at any point of
time it is enjoined on him let him give up his
office without remonstrating.

For that reason, in the charity which is

God (cf. 1 Jn. 4, 8) I beseech all my brothers whether clerical or lay, whether engaged in preaching or in prayer or in labor, to aim at keeping humble in everything; not to boast, nor be pleased with themselves nor interiorly elated, at the good words or deeds, or in fine anything good, which God says or does or accomplishes in them or through them at times, in keeping with what our Lord says, "But rejoice not at this that the spirits are subject to you" (Lk. 10, 20).

Let us know for certain that nothing but our vices and sins belong to us. And we ought to be the happier if we fall into various trials (Jas. 1, 2) and when we are enduring all sorts of distress and hardship of body and soul in this world for the sake of life everlasting.

283z. So, brothers, let us all be on our guard against any pride and vainglory. Let us keep ourselves free of the wisdom of this world and the prudence of the flesh; for it is the spirit of the flesh to want and strive hard at making words but little at accomplishing, and it is not bent on the inner religious virtue and holiness of the spirit, but wants and craves the religious virtue and holiness that shows outwardly to people. It is of such that our Lord says, "Amen I say to you, they have received their reward" (Mt. 6, 2).

The spirit of the Lord on the contrary

wants to have the flesh mortified and despised, rated low and base and worthy of
disgrace, and it strives for humility and patience, frank simplicity, and true peace of the
spirit. And always and above all it craves for
the divine fear and the divine wisdom and the
divine love of Father and Son and Holy
Ghost.

And whatever is good let us refer to the
most high and sovereign Lord God, and let us
acknowledge everything good to be his, and
for it all let us give thanks to him from whom
all good things come. As the most high,
sovereign, and only true God, let him possess
and have tendered and rendered to him
everything there is of honor and reverence,
of praise and benediction, of thanksgiving
and glory, since everything good is his by
right "who alone is good" (Lk. 18, 19).

And when we see or hear evil said or done,
or God being blasphemed, let us in word and
deed bless and praise the Lord, who is blest
forever. Amen.

18. *How the Ministers should foregather*

283-1. Each year everyone of the ministers shall be free to foregather with his
brothers wherever they may agree, on the
feast of St. Michael the Archangel, to discuss
what concerns the service of God. But all the
ministers in the region beyond the sea and

beyond the mountains should come once every three years and the rest of the ministers once every year to the chapter on the feast of Pentecost at the church of St. Mary of the Portiuncula, unless it be otherwise ordered by the minister and servant of the whole brotherhood.

19. *The brothers to live like Catholics*

283-2. All the brothers shall be Catholic and live and speak like Catholics. Should anyone, however, stray from the Catholic faith and life in speech or fact, and not amend, he should be expelled from our brotherhood. And we should regard all clergymen and all religious as our masters in what concerns the welfare of the soul and does not conflict with our religious life, and we should in the Lord be reverent toward their rank and office and their ministry.

20. *Confession and reception of the Body and Blood of our Lord by the brothers*

283-3. Let my blest brothers, both clergy and laymen, confess their sins to priests of our order. Should they not be able, let them confess to other prudent Catholic priests, firmly convinced and aware that from whichever Catholic priests they receive penance and absolution, they will be absolved beyond doubt from those sins if they take care to comply humbly and faithfully with the penance enjoined on them.

If, however, at the time they cannot have a priest, let them confess to one of their brothers, as the Apostle James says (5, 16): "Confess your sins to one another." Only, let them not for that reason fail to have recourse to the priests, because the power of binding and loosing has been given only to the priests.

Thus contrite and confessed, let them receive the body and blood of our Lord Jesus Christ with great humility and reverence, bearing in mind that the Lord himself says (Jn. 6, 55), "He who eats my flesh and drinks my blood, has life everlasting"; and (Lk. 22, 19), "Do this in remembrance of me."

21. *The praise and exhortation the brothers may give*

283-4. Whenever they please, all my brothers may with God's blessing openly give the following or a similar exhortation and act of praise among whatever people:

"Fear and honor, praise and bless, thank and adore the Lord God almighty in Trinity and Unity, the Father and the Son and the Holy Ghost, the Creator of everything. Repent (Mt. 3, 2), bring forth fruits befitting repentance (Lk. 3, 8), for mind that you are going to die soon. Give, and it shall be given to you. Forgive, and you shall be forgiven

(Lk. 6, 37-38). And, if you do not forgive people their sins, the Lord will not forgive you your sins (cf. Mk. 11, 26). Confess all your sins (Jas. 5, 16). Blessed are they who die in repentance, for they will be in the kingdom of Heaven. Woe to those who do not die in repentance, for they will be children of the Devil, whose works they do (cf. Jn. 8, 44), and will go into everlasting fire. Beware and refrain from all evil, and persevere to the end in what is good.

22. *Words of guidance for the brothers*

283-5. Let us, brothers all, take note that our Lord says, "Love your enemies and do good to those who hate you" (Mt. 5, 44). For also our Lord Jesus Christ, whose footsteps we should follow (1 Pet. 2, 21), called his betrayer friend and offered himself voluntarily to his crucifiers. All therefore who unjustly put on us trial and distress, shame and insult, grief and pain of various kinds together with martyrdom and death, are our friends, whom we ought to love much, because through what they put on us we obtain life everlasting.

And let us hate our person with its vices and sins, because with its carnal way of living it would deprive us of the love of our Lord Jesus Christ and of life everlasting while sending itself and everything else to Hell; for it is our fault if we prove foul and vile, averse to virtue, but ready and willing for evil, since, as our Lord says in the Gospel: It is from the heart of people that their evil designs arise and come forth, their adulteries, fornications, murders, thefts, deeds of avarice and guile, deceit, shamelessness, the jealous eye, false witnessing, blasphemies, pride, and folly (cf. Mt. 15, 19; Mk. 7, 21). All these evils come forth from within, from the heart of a man, and they are what defiles a person (ib.).

Now, however, after we have left the world, there is nothing else for us to do but be concerned about following the will of our Lord and pleasing him. Let us be very careful not to be soil that is along the wayside, or that is stony and thorny, according to what our Lord says in the Gospel, "The seed is the word of God. But what fell at the wayside and was trodden under foot, are those who hear the word and do not appreciate it, and soon the Devil comes and snatches up what has been sown in their hearts and removes the word from their hearts, lest they believe and be saved. But what fell on stony ground are those who on hearing the word, quickly welcome it with joy, but when tribulation and persecution arise, they are soon scandalized at the word, and they have no root within but they are inconstant, because they believe for a while and fall away in the time of trial. But what fell among the thorns, are those who listen to the word of God, and then concern and the worries of this world, and the delusion of riches, and appetites regarding other things come in and choke the word, and it is made fruitless. But what was sown in good ground, are those who, listening to the word with a good and most favorably disposed heart, appreciate it and treasure it, and bring forth fruit in due time" (cf. Mt. 13; Mk. 4, Lk. 8).

283-6. For that reason, brothers, we should, as the Lord says, let the dead bury the dead (Mt. 8, 22). And let us be well on our guard against the spite and cunning of Satan, who wants man not to keep his mind and heart directed toward the Lord God, and goes about with the desire of ravishing the heart of a person under the pretext of some compensation or advantage, and of snuffing the word and the commandments of the Lord from his mind, and he wants to make a person's heart blind with worldly affairs and care, and wants to live in it, as the Lord says: "When an unclean spirit has gone out of a man, he wanders about desert and waterless places in search of rest, and finding none, he says: I will go back into my house, which I left. And coming to it, he finds it empty, swept clean, and in order. Then he goes and takes along seven other spirits worse than himself, and they come in and live there, and the last state of that man proves worse than the first" (cf. Mt. 12, Lk. 11).

So, brothers all, let us keep a close guard on ourselves, lest under the pretext of some compensation or of work or advantage we let our mind and heart stray or be withdrawn from the Lord. But in the holy charity which is God (1 Jn. 4, 16) I beseech all the brothers, the ministers as well as the rest, that, removing every hindrance and disregarding all care and concern, they should the best way they can, serve, love, adore and honor the Lord God with a clean heart and a pure intention, which is what he seeks above all.

283-7. And always let us make a home and dwelling within us for him, the Lord God almighty, Father and Son and Holy Ghost, who says: "Watch, therefore, and pray all the time, so that you may be found worthy to escape all the evils which are to come, and to stand before the Son of Man" (cf. Lk. 21, 36). And when you are about to pray (Lk. 18, 1), say, "Our Father, who are in Heaven."

And let us adore him with a pure heart, because we must always pray and not lose heart (Lk. 18, 1), for the Father seeks such to worship him. "God is a spirit, and those who worship him, must worship him in spirit and

in truth" (Jn. 4, 23). And let us have recourse
to him "as the shepherd and guardian of our
souls" (1 Pet. 2, 25). who says: "I am the
good shepherd, who feed my sheep and give
my life for my sheep" (Jn. 10). But you all
are brothers. And call no one on earth your
father, for one is your Father, who is in
Heaven. And do not be called master, for
one is your Master, who is in Heaven, the
Christ (cf. Mt. 23). "If you remain in me,
and my words remain in you, ask for whatever you wish and it shall be done to you"
(Jn. 15, 7). "Wherever two or three are
gathered in my name, there am I in the midst
of them" (Mt. 15, 20). "Behold, I am with
you all days even to the consummation of
the world" (Mt. 28, 20). "The words I have
spoken to you, are spirit and life" (Jn. 6, 64).
"I am the way, the truth, and the life"
(Jn. 14, 6).

283-8. So let us hold fast to his words, his
life and doctrine, and his holy Gospel, for he
has deigned to pray to his Father for us and
to manifest his name to us, saying: "Father,
I have manifested your name to the men
you have given me . . . because the words you
have given to me I have given to them. And
they have received them, and have known
truly that I have come forth from you, and
they have believed that you have sent me. I

pray for them; not for the world do I pray, but for those whom you have given me, because they are yours, and everything that is mine is yours . . . Holy Father, keep in your name those whom you have given me, that they may be one just as we are. . . . These things I speak in the world, in order that they may have my joy made full in them. I have given them your word, and the world has hated them, because they are not of the world, just as I am not of the world. I do not pray that you take them out of the world, but that you keep them from evil. . . . Sanctify them in the truth. Your word is truth. Just as you have sent me into the world, so I have sent them into the world, and for them I sanctify myself, that they also may be sanctified in truth. Yet not for these only do I pray, but for those also who through their word are to believe in me, . . . that they may be perfected in unity, and that the world may know that you have sent me and have loved them just as you have loved me. . . . And I will make your name known to them, in order that the love with which you have loved me, may be in them and I in them. . . . Father, I wish that where I am, they also whom you have given me may be with me, that they may behold your glory in your kingdom" (cf. Jn. 17, 6 on).

23. Prayer, praise and thanksgiving

283-9. Almighty, most high, most holy and sovereign God, holy and just Father, Lord King of heaven and earth, for your very self we give you thanks, because by your holy will and through your only Son in the Holy Spirit you have created everything spiritual and corporal, and you placed us, made according to your image and likeness, in Paradise, and it was through our fault that we fell.

And we give you thanks because, just as you created us through your Son, so in that true and holy love with which you have loved us, did you have him, true God and true man, be born of the glorious and most blessed holy Mary ever virgin, and wish us captives to be redeemed through his cross and blood and death.

And we give you thanks because this your Son is to come again in the glory of his majesty to send to the eternal fire those accursed ones who did not practice repentance and did not acknowledge you; but to say to everybody that did acknowledge, adore and serve you in repentance, "Come, you blest of my Father, take over the kingdom prepared for you from the beginning of the world" (Mt. 25, 34).

And since we wretched sinners all are not fit to mention your name, we implore insistently that our Lord Jesus Christ, your beloved Son, in whom you were well pleased, may together with the Holy Ghost the Paraclete give you such thanks as please you and them for everything—for he ever suffices you in every regard, through whom you have done so much for us. Alleluja.

And for the sake of your love we humbly beg our glorious Mother, the most blessed Mary ever virgin; the blessed Michael, Gabriel, Raphael and all the choirs of the blessed spirits, of the seraphim, cherubim and thrones, of the dominations, principalities and powers, of the virtues, archangels and angels; the blessed John the Baptist, John the Evangelist, Peter, Paul, and the blessed patriarchs, prophets, innocents, apostles, evangelists, disciples, martyrs, confessors, virgins; the blessed Elias and Henoch, and all the saints who ever were or shall be or are, that they may give such thanks as please you for all these things, to you, the true, sovereign, eternal, and living God, together with your dearest Son our Lord Jesus Christ, and the Holy Ghost the Paraclete forevermore. Amen. Alleluja.

283-10. And all who within the holy Catholic and Apostolic Church wish to serve God the Lord; and all the ecclesiastical orders, priests, deacons, subdeacons, acolytes, exorcists, lectors, ostiaries, and all the clergy; all the religious both men and women; all boys and girls and little children, the poor and needy, kings and princes, laborers, farmers, servants and masters; all virgins and continent and married women, all lay men and women; all infants, growing people, youths and old people, the healthy and the sick; all persons of low and high rank; and all peoples, races, tribes and tongues, all nations and all men all over the world now and to come—all we lesser brothers and useless servants humbly beg and entreat them that all of us may persevere in the true faith and in repentance, for there is no other way for anybody to be saved.

With all our heart and soul and mind and strength and fortitude and understanding and all our faculties: with all our endeavor, affection, and yearning: with all we desire and will, let us all love God the Lord, who has given and still gives us all our whole body, soul and life; who has created and redeemed us and only in his mercy will save us; who has done and keeps doing everything good to us, miserable and wretched, corrupt and foul ,ungrateful and wicked as we are.

So let us desire nothing else, wish for nothing else, take pleasure and delight in nothing else but our Creator, Redeemer and Savior, the only true God, who is the perfect good, everything good, wholly good, the true and sovereign good; he who alone is good (Lk. 18, 19), loving and gentle, sweet and lovable; he who alone is holy, just, true and fair; who alone is kind, innocent and clean; from whom, and through whom, and in whom is all pardon, all grace, and all glory for all the repentant and the just and for all the blessed rejoicing together in Heaven.

Then let nothing hinder us, nothing keep us apart, nothing get in the way. All over, everywhere, at every hour and at any time, day after day and without ceasing let us all believe in him with a true and humble faith, cherish him in our heart, and love, honor, adore, serve, praise and bless him, glorify, exalt and extol him, and give thanks to him, the most high, sovereign, eternal God, in Trinity and Unity, Father, Son and Holy Ghost, the Creator of all things, the Savior of all who have faith and hope and love for him; who is without beginning and without end, unchangeable, invisible, unutterable, ineffable, incomprehensible, unfathomable, blest, worthy of praise, glorious, exalted above all, sublime, supreme, yet sweet, lovable, delightful, and always altogether desirable beyond everything forever and ever.

In the name of the Lord I beseech all the brothers to learn the text and sense of what is written down in this rule of life for the salvation of our soul, and often to call it to mind. And I implore God that he the omnipotent, who is threefold and single, may bless all who teach, learn, recall and practice these points every time they repeat and do what is here written down for our salvation. And I entreat all, while kissing their feet, greatly to love, watch over and treasure these articles.

And on the part of almighty God and the Lord Pope as well as in obedience I, Brother Francis, strictly command and enjoin that in what is written down in this rule of life no one subtract anything nor add any further written word to it, nor shall the brothers have any other rule.

Glory be to the Father and to the Son and to the Holy Ghost, as it was in the beginning, is now and ever shall be, world without end. Amen.

284. The present rule of the Friars Minor, in more compact form than the first, has served a vast order as its direct inspiration for more than seven hundred years. It is basic for the observances of the Friars Minor or Franciscans simply so called, the Friars Minor Conventual, and the Friars Minor Capuchin. Changes in application have become necessary in these centuries, other changes have been deemed necessary, but the rule itself remains, to be observed to the letter as conditions allow, to be observed in spirit at all times:

PRESENT RULE
OF THE FRIARS MINOR

1. *In the name of the Lord begins the life of the Friars Minor*

The rule and life of the Lesser Brethren is this, namely to observe the holy Gospel of our Lord Jesus Christ, by living in obedience, without property, and in chastity. Brother Francis promises obedience and reverence to the lord Pope Honorius and his successors canonically entering office, and to the Roman Church. And let the rest of the brothers be bound to obey Brother Francis and his successors.

2. *On those who wish to take up this life and how they are to be received*

284a. If any persons wish to take up this rule and come to our brothers, they should send them to their provincial ministers, to whom alone and no one else the authority to accept brothers may be granted. Let the ministers in turn examine them carefully on the Catholic Faith and the sacraments of the Church. And if they believe all these things and are minded to profess them faithfully and observe them firmly to the last; and if they are unmarried, or if they are married and the wives have already entered a convent or after taking a vow of continence have with the authority of the diocesan bishop given them the permission, and the wives are of such an age that no suspicion can arise concerning them: let the ministers tell them what the Holy Gospel says (Mt. 19, 21), that they should go and sell all they have and endeavor to distribute it to the poor. If they cannot do the latter, their good intention suffices.

And let the brothers and their ministers take care not to be concerned about their temporal affairs, so that they may freely do with their property whatever the Lord inspires them. If, however, advice be sought, the ministers shall be free to send them to some God-fearing persons at whose advice their goods may be distributed to the poor.

Thereafter let them give them the clothes of probation, to wit, two tunics without a capuche, a cincture, drawers, and a chaperon reaching to the cincture, unless said ministers should ever find something else advisable according to God.

When, however, the year of probation is ended, they are to be accepted for obedience, promising always to observe this life and rule. And at the command of the Lord Pope it shall by no means be permitted them to leave this order, because, according to the holy Gospel, nobody putting his hand to the plow and looking backward is fit for the kingdom of God (Lk. 9, 62).

And those who have promised obedience,

shall have one tunic with a capuche and, such as wish, another without a capuche.

And those who are forced by necessity, may wear shoes. And all the brothers shall dress in garments of low value and they may patch them with sacking and other patches with the blessing of God. And I admonish and exhort them not to despise or judge people whom they see dressed in soft and showy garments and using choice food and drink, but rather let everyone judge and despise himself.

3. *On the Divine Office and fasting and how the brothers should behave in the world*

284b. Let the clerics say the Divine Office according to the custom of the holy Roman Church, excepting the Psalter; for that reason they may have breviaries. The lay brothers shall say 24 Our Fathers for the Matins, five for the Lauds, seven each for Prime, Tierce, Sext and None, for the Vespers twelve, and seven for the Compline; and let them pray for the dead.

And they shall fast from the feast of All Saints until the Nativity of our Lord. As to the holy forty-day fast which goes on for forty continuous days after Epiphany and which the Lord consecrated with his holy fast, let those who keep it of their free will be blest be the Lord, and those who do not wish, should not be obliged to it. But they must fast thy other forty-day fast until the Resurrection of our Lord. At other times, however, they should not be bound to fast except on Friday. But in time of manifest necessity the brothers should not be held to corporal fasting.

But I advise, warn and exhort my brothers in the Lord Jesus Christ that when they go about in the world they do not become involved in disputes and wordy contentions, nor judge others, but let them be meek, peaceable and reserved, gentle and humble, speaking courteously to everybody as is proper. And they are not to ride horseback unless forced to by manifest necessity or infirmity. Into whatever house they enter, let them first say, Peace to this house. And according to the holy Gospel, they shall be free to eat of whatever foods are put before them.

4. *The brothers are not to accept money*

284c. I firmly command all the brothers that they must not in any way accept coins or money, either themselves or through an intermediary person. Still, for the needs of the sick and for the clothing of the rest of the brothers, let the ministers and custodes alone take attentive care through spiritual friends as will seem to them suitable to the requirement of place, time and cold climate; saving always that, as has been said, they may not accept coins or money.

5. On the manner of working

284d. Those brothers whom the Lord has given the grace of working, should work faithfully and devotedly in such a way that with idleness, the enemy of the soul, excluded, they do not extinguish the spirit of holy prayer and devotion, to which everything else temporal must give service. In return for their labor they may accept for themselves and their brothers what is needful for the body, except coins or money, and that humbly as is proper for servants of God and the followers of the most holy poverty.

6. That the brothers shall appropriate nothing to themselves, on seeking alms and on the sick brothers

284e. The brothers are to take nothing as their own, neither house, nor place, nor anything. And as pilgrims and strangers in this world, while serving the Lord in poverty and humility let them go confidently in quest of alms; and they ought not be ashamed of it, because the Lord made himself poor in this world for our sake. This is that peak of highest poverty which has established you who are my dearest brothers as heirs and kings of the kingdom of Heaven; it has made you poor in possessions but raised you high in virtues. Let that be your portion, as it leads to the land of the living (Ps. 141, 7). May you, most beloved brothers, attach yourselves altogether to it, and wish in the name of our Lord Jesus Christ to have nothing else under Heaven forevermore.

And wherever the brothers are located or meet one another, let them act toward one another like members of a family. And each should with assurance make his need known to another; for, if a mother tends and loves her child in the flesh, with how much greater attention must anybody love and tend his brother in the spirit? And if anyone of them falls into illness, the rest of the brothers must wait on him as they themselves would want to be waited on.

7. *On the penance to be imposed on brothers who sin*

284f. If any of the brothers at the instigation of the Enemy, should sin mortally, in the case of those sins regarding which it has been ordained among the brothers that recourse may be had to the provinical ministers only, said brothers are bound to have recourse to them as soon as they can, without delay. The ministers in turn, if they are priests, should with mercy impose a penance on them, but if they are not priests, they should have it imposed by other priests of the order as they may judge most expedient under God.

And they must take care lest they be angry or disturbed over anybody's sin, because anger and agitation hinder charity in themselves and others.

8. *On electing the Minister General of this brotherhood, and the Pentecost chapter*

284g. All the brothers shall be bound always to have one of the brothers of this order as the minister general and servant of the whole brotherhood and shall be strictly bound to obey him. At his passing the election of a successor must be made by the provincial ministers and custodes in the Pentecost chapter, for which the ministers provincial shall be bound always to foregather wherever it may have been appointed by the minister general, and that once in three years or at a longer or shorter interval as may be ordained by said minister. And if at any time it should become apparent to the whole of the provincial ministers and custodes that said minister is not competent for the service and general welfare of the brothers, said brothers who are charged with the election, shall be bound in the name of the Lord to elect a different brother as their custos. After the Pentecost chapter in turn the ministers and custodes severally may if they wish and find it advisable convoke their brothers for a chapter once the same year in their own custodies.

9. *On preachers*

284h. The brothers shall not preach in the see of any bishop when it may have been refused to them by him. And let no one of the brothers dare to preach at all to the people unless he has been examined and approved and has had the charge of preaching granted to him by the minister general of this brotherhood. I further warn and exhort these same brothers that in the preaching they do, their words be fire-tried and refined (Ps. 11, 7), to serve for the benefit and edification of the people, telling them about the vices and virtues, the punishment and glory in few words, for a speedy word did the Lord make on earth (Rom. 8).

10. *On admonishing and correcting the brothers*

284i. The brothers who are the ministers and servants of the other brothers, shall visit and admonish their brothers and correct them humbly and charitably, not enjoining on them anything that may injure their soul or our rule. In turn the brothers who are subjects, should recall that for God's sake they have renounced their own will. Wherefore, I command them strictly to obey their ministers in everything which they have promised the Lord to observe and which is not against their soul and our rule. And wherever there are brothers who may know and be convinced that they cannot keep the rule spiritually, let them have the duty and the opportunity to recur to their ministers. The ministers, however, should receive them with charity and kindness and treat them with such fellowship that they can speak and act toward them like masters toward their servants; for so it ought to be that the ministers be the servants of all the brothers.

I further warn and exhort the brothers in the Lord Jesus Christ that they beware of all pride, vainglory, envy, avarice, of interest and concern about this world, of detraction and murmuring. And let not the unlettered be concerned about learning, but let them mind that above everything else they should desire to have the spirit of the Lord and his holy operation, to pray to him always with a pure heart, to have humility, patience amid persecution and infirmity, and love for those who persecute, reproach and accuse us, because the Lord has said: Love your enemies and pray for those who persecute and slander you (Mt. 5, 44). Blessed are they who suffer persecution for the sake of justice, for theirs is the kingdom of Heaven (Mt. 5, 10). But he who perseveres to the last, shall be saved (Mt. 10, 22).

11. *The brothers are not to enter the monasteries of nuns*

284j. I strictly command all the brothers not to have suspicious associations or conversations with women; and that they do not enter the monasteries of nuns, except the brothers to whom special permission has been given by the Apostolic See. Nor should they become godfathers of men or women, lest on that account scandal should arise among the brothers or concerning the brothers.

12. *On those going among the Saracens and other non-believers*

284k. Whoever of the brothers may wish on Divine inspiration to go among the Saracens and other non-believers should ask leave for it from their provincial ministers. But the ministers must give permission to go to none but such as they see are fit to be sent.

Furthermore, I enjoin on the ministers by obedience that they ask of the Lord Pope one of the cardinals of the holy Roman Church to be governor, protector and corrector of this brotherhood: so that submissive and subject always at the feet of the same holy Church, grounded in the Catholic faith (Col. 1, 23) we may, as we have firmly promised, observe the poverty and the humility and the Holy Gospel of our Lord Jesus Christ.

285. Unlike the first and the second rule of the Friars Minor, the rule taken as basic by Poor Clare groups is not the immediate, so to say holographic, work of St. Francis. It comes to us in the person of St. Clare herself, for whom it was approved by Innocent IV on August 9, 1253. Yet nobody will doubt that it hews close to the spirit and even the letter of what St. Francis prescribed in his day. The wording is identical in entire passages with the rule of the Friars. St. Clare was too loyal to St. Francis to depart from his spirit. She testifies in her rule itself to her adhering to the directions of St. Francis. Our text omits the ceremonial preamble and conclusion.

THE RULE OF THE POOR CLARES

1. *In the name of the Lord, amen, the Rule beginneth:*

The form of life of the Order of Poor Sisters, which the blessed Francis founded, is this: to observe the holy Gospel of our Lord Jesus Christ by living in obedience, without property, and in chastity.

Clare, unworthy handmaid of Jesus Christ and little plant of our most blessed father Francis, promises obedience and reverence to the Lord Pope Innocent and his canonically entering successors, and to the Roman Church. And as in the beginning of her conversion she together with her sisters promised obedience to the blessed Francis, so does she promise to observe it unfailingly toward his successors. And the rest of the sisters shall be bound always to obey the successors of the blessed Francis, and Sister Clare, and the other canonically elected abbesses succeeding her.

2. *On those who wish to take up this life and how they are to be received*

285a. If anyone at Divine inspiration comes to us wishing to take up this life, the abbess shall be bound to seek the consent of all the sisters, and if the majority consent, she may receive her, with the permission of our Lord Cardinal Protector.

If she sees fit to receive her, she should carefully examine her, or have her examined, on the Catholic Faith and the sacraments of the Church. And if she believes all these things and is willing faithfully to confess them and firmly to observe them to the end; and if she has no husband or, if she has and he has already entered an order on the authority of the diocesan bishop after making the vow of continence; and also if advanced age or any ailment or mental failure do not interfere with her observance of this life: then let the tenor of our life be carefully explained to her.

And if she proves suitable, let the words of the holy Gospel be told her: that she should go and sell everything she has and endeavor to give it to the poor. But if she is unable to do that, her good will suffices for her.

And the abbess and her sisters shall beware not to be concerned about her temporal goods, so that she can freely do about her property whatever the Lord will inspire her. But if advice is sought, they may send her to some discreet God-fearing persons at whose advice her goods should be distributed to the poor.

After her hair has been cut off roundabout and her secular garb has been laid aside, let the abbess give her three tunics and a mantle. Thereafter she shall not be permitted to go outside the monastery except for a useful, reasonable, evident and commendable cause.

When, however, the year of probation is ended, she shall be received for obedience, promising to observe forever this life and pattern of our poverty.

No one is to have the veil within the time of probation.

The sisters may also have mantelets for the sake of ease and decency about their service and work. The abbess, however, shall make discreet provision for them regarding clothes according to their personal constitution as well as to places and seasons and cold climates, as she will find it suiting to their need.

Girls received into the monastery under the limit of the canonical age shall be shorn roundabout and, putting off their secular garb, be dressed in religious apparel as the abbess sees fit. But when they reach the legitimate age, they shall make their profession dressed in the manner of the rest.

And for them as well as for the rest of the novices the abbess shall provide a mistress from among the more discerning sisters of the entire monastery, who shall carefully instruct them in holy living and proper habits suited to the nature of our profession.

No woman is to take up residence within the monastery unless she has been received according to the pattern of our profession.

And for love of the most holy and beloved Child, who was wrapped in poor little scraps and laid in the manger, and for love of his most holy Mother, I admonish, beseech and exhort my sisters always to dress in cheap garments.

3. *On Divine Office, fasting, confession and communion*

285b. The sisters who can read shall recite the Divine Office according to the custom of the Friars Minor, for which reason they may have breviaries; the Office is to be read without singing it. And the sisters who for reasonable cause at times may not be able to say their Hours by reading them, may say the Our Father like other sisters.

The sisters, however, who cannot read, shall say 24 Our Fathers for the Matins, five for the Lauds, seven for each of the Hours of Prime, Tierce, Sext and None, for the Vespers twelve, and for the Compline seven. For the dead, too, they shall say seven Our Fathers with the Eternal Rest at Vespers and twelve at Matins, while the literate sisters are bound to say the Office of the Dead. When a sister of our monastery dies, they shall say 50 Our Fathers.

The sisters shall fast at all times. But on the Nativity of our Lord, no matter on what day it occurs, they may take two meals. The abbess shall as she sees fit leniently dispense in the case of the young, the frail, and those serving outside of the enclosure. In time of evident need, however, the sisters shall not be held to bodily fasting.

At least twelve times a year the sisters shall go to confession at the permission of the abbess. On such occasions they must take care not to bring up matters other than what pertains to confession and the welfare of their soul.

They shall go to Communion on seven occasions, namely Christmas, Thursday of Holy Week, the Resurrection of our Lord, Pentecost, the Assumption of the Blessed Virgin, the feast of St. Francis, and the feast of All Saints. The chaplain may be permitted to celebrate within the monastery to give holy Communion to sisters well or ill.

4. *Election and office of the abbess, chapter, officials*

285c. The sisters are bound to observe the canonical form in electing the abbess. They shall, too, take care in plenty of time to have the Minister General or Provincial of the Friars Minor instruct them with the word of God toward complete harmony and the benefit of the community in making the election.

Only a professed sister shall be elected. And if a non-professed sister should be elected or otherwise appointed, obedience shall not be given her unless first she professes the form of our poverty. On her passing, the election of another abbess is to be held.

And if at any time it should be apparent to the totality of the sisters that the aforesaid abbess is unequal to their service and common benefit, the aforesaid sisters shall as soon as possible elect another sister in the aforesaid form as their abbess and mother.

Let the sister elected, however, give thought to the character of the burden she has undertaken, and to Whom she must give an account of the flock committed to her. Let her endeavor to preside over the rest by her virtues and holy habits rather than by her office, so that inspired by her example, the sisters may obey her out of love rather than fear.

She should beware of private preferences, lest by too much favor toward any part she beget scandal for the entirety. Let her comfort the afflicted. Let her, too, be the last refuge of those under trial, lest, if the wholesome remedies are wanting in her, the malady of despair prevail in the weak.

She shall observe the common life in everything, but especially in church, dormitory, refectory, infirmary, and in clothing. Her vicar also is bound to observe the same in like manner.

At least once a week the abbess shall be bound to convoke her sisters for chapter, in which she as well as the sisters must make humble confession of ordinary public offenses and omissions. And whatever needs to be dealt with for the benefit and good name of the monastery, she should discuss there with all her sisters; for often the Lord reveals what is best to the least.

No heavy debt should be contracted except by common consent of the sisters and upon evident necessity; and it must be done through a procurator.

Let the abbess, however, together with her sisters beware of accepting any deposit in the monastery, for disturbances and scandals often arise from things of the sort.

In order to safeguard the unity of mutual charity and peace, let all the office-holders of the monastery be elected by common consent of all the sisters. In the same way let at least eight of the more discreet sisters be elected whose advice the abbess is bound always to consult in matters which our form of life requires.

5. Silence, parlor, grille

285d. From the hour of the Compline to the Tierce the sisters shall maintain silence, excepting those who serve outside of the monastery. They shall always keep silence in church, in the dormitory, and, at mealtime only, in the refectory, not, however, in the infirmary, where for the recreation and service of the sick the sisters may always speak with discretion. Yet they can always and everywhere indicate briefly and in a subdued voice what may be necessary.

The sisters are not allowed to converse in the parlor or at the grille without the permission of the abbess or her vicar. And those having permission must not presume to converse in the parlor except in the presence and the hearing of two sisters. But they must not presume to go to the grille except in the presence of at least three sisters appointed by the abbess or her vicar from among the eight discreets elected to the abbess's council by all the sisters.

The abbess and her vicar are bound in their own case to follow this procedure in conversation.

Such permission for the grille shall be given very rarely; never at all for the portal.

Inside the grille a curtain shall be put up, to be moved aside only when the word of God is preached there, or if any sister were to converse with anybody.

The grille shall be provided also with a wooden door fortified in the best way possible with two different iron locks as well as hinges and bars, so that especially at night it can be locked with two keys, of which the abbess is to keep one and the sacristan the other; and the grille shall remain locked at all times except when the Divine Office is being attended and for the reasons mentioned above.

No sister must under any condition speak with anybody at the grille before sunrise or after sunset.

At the parlor in turn a curtain shall remain put up on the interior, and it is not to be moved aside.

In the fast of St. Martin and the great Lent no sister shall speak to anybody in the parlor except to the priest for the sake of confession or another manifest need, which shall be reserved to the prudent judgment of the abbess or her vicar.

6. *Having no property*

285e. After the most high heavenly Father deigned to enlighten my heart with his grace to do penance upon the example and direction of our most blessed father St. Francis, shortly after his own conversion I together with my sisters of our own accord promised him obedience. When our blessed father, in turn, saw that we feared neither poverty, hardship, trial, nor the low regard and scorn of the world, but rather held them to be great delights, in his pity he wrote down a pattern of life for us after this fashion:

"Since on Divine inspiration you have made yourselves daughters and handmaids of the most high sovereign King and Father in Heaven, and have espoused yourselves to the Holy Ghost, by choosing to live according to the Holy Gospel in its perfection: therefore it is my will and promise, in my name and that of my brothers, always to take the same diligent care and special responsibility for you as for them."

As long as he lived he fulfilled that pledge carefully, and it was his will that it be fulfilled at all times by the Friars. And so that we as well as those who were to come after us might never depart from the most holy poverty we have embraced, shortly before his death he again wrote down his last will for us, saying:

"I, little brother Francis, want to pursue the life and poverty of our most high Lord Jesus Christ and his most holy Mother, and to persevere in it to the last. And I beg you, my ladies, and advise you to live forever in that most holy life and poverty. And be well on your guard lest you ever in any way depart from it at the advice or instruction of anybody."

And as I together with my sisters have always been concerned to safeguard the holy poverty we have promised God our Lord and the blessed Francis, so let the abbesses who will succeed me in office and all the sisters to the last observe it inviolably, that is to say:

That they do not, personally or through an intermediary, accept or hold any possession or property, or even anything that would reasonably be termed a property right, except for as much ground as necessity requires to insure decency and seclusion for the monastery, and such ground is not to be cultivated except as a garden for their own need.

7. Manner of working

285f. The sisters to whom the Lord has given the grace of working, shall, after the hour of the Tierce, proceed to work faithfully and devotedly at some handicraft that is becoming and useful to all, in such a way that excluding idleness as the enemy of the soul they do not extinguish the spirit of holy prayer and devotion, to which all other things temporal must give service.

The abbess or her vicar shall be bound to assign what manual work they are to do, in the chapter, where all are present.

The same is to be done should any alms be sent in for the needs of the sisters by any people, so that commendation of the donors can be made in common. And all such alms shall be distributed for the benefit of all by the abbess or her vicar with the advice of the discreets.

8. *On renouncing property, on begging, on the infirm*

285g. The sisters are to appropriate nothing to themselves, neither house, nor place, nor any thing, and as pilgrims and strangers in this world who are serving the Lord in poverty and humility, they shall with confidence send out for alms.

Nor should they be ashamed to do so, because the Lord made himself poor for us in this world. This is that height of most sublime poverty which has established you, my dearest sisters, as heirs and queens of the kingdom of Heaven, has made you poor in material things but has exalted you in virtues. Let this be your portion, for it leads you to the land of the living. And do you, dearest sisters, clinging to it with all your might, desire to have nothing else under heaven forever in the name of our Lord Jesus Christ and his most holy Mother.

No sister shall be permitted to send any letter, or to accept anything, or to give anything away outside of the monastery without the permission of the abbess. Nor is she allowed to have anything that the abbess has not given her or permitted her to have.

Should anything be sent to her by her parents or by other people, the abbess shall have it given to her. She in turn may use it if she has need of it; if not, she should in charity bestow it on a sister who needs it. If, however, any money has been transmitted to her, the abbess shall on the advice of the discreets see that she be provided with things she needs.

As to ailing sisters, the abbess shall be firmly bound to inquire concernedly, in person and through other sisters, what their ailment requires both in point of advice and of foods and other necessaries, and likewise to provide for them in charity and mercy as far as the place can afford it; because all are bound to serve and provide for their ailing sisters just as they would wish to be waited on if they were confined by any ailment.

Each should with assurance make her need known to the other. And if a mother loves and nourishes her daughter in the flesh, how much the more concernedly must a sister love and nourish her sister in the spirit.

The sick may rest on straw-ticks and have a feather pillow for a head rest, and those who need it may use woolen footwear and quilted coverlets.

When the aforesaid ailing sisters are visited by persons entering the monastery, they are permitted singly to reply with a few kind words to those speaking to them. But other sisters having permission shall not presume to speak to people entering the monastery except in the presence and hearing of two sisters discreet designated by the abbess or her vicar. The abbess and her vicar shall be bound to the same procedure for conversation.

9. *Penance for delinquents and rules for externe sisters*

285h. If any sister at the instigation of the Enemy should sin mortally against the form of our profession and not amend after being admonished two or three times by the abbess or other sisters, she shall make her meals of bread and water seated on the floor before all the sisters in the refectory for as many days as she remains obstinate, and if the abbess sees fit she shall subject her to heavier penalty.

While she remains obstinate, let prayer be said for her that the Lord may enlighten her heart toward penance.

The abbess in turn and her sisters must take care not to get angry or agitated on account of anyone's sin, because anger and agitation in them and others interfere with charity.

Should it happen, which God forbid, that ever an occasion of agitation or scandal develop from word or manner between sister and sister, let the sister who gave cause for the agitation, promptly, before she offers the Lord the gift of her prayer, not only prostrate herself humbly at the feet of the other to ask pardon, but also in all simplicity beg her to intercede with the Lord for her that he may forgive her. The offended sister, mindful of the words of our Lord, "Unless you forgive from your heart, neither will your heavenly Father forgive you," shall freely forgive her sister any wrong she has done her.

The sisters who serve outside of the monastery shall make no long delay abroad unless some reason of evident necessity should demand it. And they must go about modestly and speak little, so that they can always edify beholders. And they shall not be sponsors for men or women, lest it become an occasion of complaint or disorder.

And they should not dare to report the gossip of the world in the monastery. And they shall be firmly bound not to relate outside of the monastery anything said or done within, that might cause scandal. Should any sister have failed in these two particulars from lack of forethought, it shall rest with the prudent judgment of the abbess to impose a merciful penance on her. But if it resulted from a bad habit, the abbess on the advice of her discreets should impose a penance suited to the quality of the guilt.

10. *Admonition and correction*

285i. The abbess shall direct and visit her sisters and correct them with humility and charity, not bidding them to do anything that would be against their conscience and the form of our profession.

The sisters in turn who are subject, should remember that for God's sake they have renounced their own will. Therefore they shall be firmly bound to obey their abbess in everything which they have promised the Lord to observe and which is not contrary to their soul and our profession.

The abbess, however, should deal so familiarly with them that they can speak and act toward her like a mistress to her servant.

For so it must be that the abbess is the servant of all the sisters.

But I admonish and exhort the sisters in
the Lord Jesus Christ that they take heed
against all pride, vainglory, envy, avarice,
care and concern for this world, detraction
and murmuring, dissension and division.
Rather let them always be concerned to preserve among themselves that unity of mutual
charity which is the bond of perfection.

And let those ignorant of letters not be
eager to learn them. But let them mind that
above all else they must have the Spirit of the
Lord and his holy operation, to pray to him
always with a pure heart and to have humility and patience amid trial and infirmity,
and to love those who persecute, censure and
accuse us, for the Lord says, "Blessed are
those who suffer persecution for justice' sake,
for theirs is the kingdom of Heaven. But he
who perseveres to the last shall be saved."

11. *Enclosure*

285j. The porter shall be mature in character, and of a suitable age. During the day
she shall remain at her place in a little open
cell that is doorless. A competent companion
should likewise be assigned to her, who if
need be shall take her place in everything.

The door, however, shall be fortified in the
best way possible with two different iron locks

as well as hinges and bars, so that especially at night it can be locked with two keys, of which the porter is to keep one and the abbess the other. And during the day it shall never be left unguarded and shall be securely locked with one key. And they should take the most studious heed and care that at no time the door be left standing open any more than can becomingly be helped. Nor shall it be opened at all for anybody wanting to come in except for a person having permission from the Holy See or from our Lord Cardinal.

Nor shall the sisters let anybody enter the monastery before sunrise or remain it it after sunset unless an evident, reasonable, and unavoidable cause demands it.

If on occasion of blessing the abbess, or professing any sister or nun, or for any other reason, a bishop shall have gotten leave to celebrate Mass within, he should rest content to appear with as few and respectable companions and attendants as possible.

Whenever it is necessary for people to come inside the monastery to do any work, let the abbess be concerned to put a suitable person at the door who shall open it only to those appointed for the work and no others.

All the sisters shall take most studious care at such time not to be seen by those entering.

12. *Visitor, Chaplain, Cardinal Protector*

285k. Our Visitor shall always be a member of the Order of Friars Minor at the will and command of our Cardinal. He should be a person such that of his good name and character there be full knowledge.

It shall be his duty to correct, in head as well as in members, any transgressions committed against the form of our profession.

Taking a position in public, so that he can be seen by the rest, he may speak with groups and individuals on what pertains to his office of visitation as he shall judge most expedient.

For the love of God and the blessed Francis we ask the Order of Friars Minor to allow us the favor of a chaplain with a clerical companion of good reputation and thoughtful discretion, and two lay brothers who are friends of a life of holiness and propriety, to be of assistance to us in our poverty, as we have always had it through the mercy of said Order of Friars Minor.

It shall not be permitted the chaplain to enter the monastery without a companion, and when they enter, they shall stay in a public place in sight of each other and of others. It shall be permitted them to enter for the confession of the ailing who may not be able to go to the parlor, and for bringing them Communion and Extreme Unction, and for making the commendation of their soul.

For funerals and solemn Masses of the dead, for digging or opening a grave or also putting it in order, a sufficient number of competent persons may enter at the abbess's discretion.

Moreover, the sisters shall be firmly bound always to have as our governor, protector and protector that Cardinal of the Holy Roman Church who has been appointed by the Lord Pope for the Friars Minor, so that, ever submissive and subject at the feet of the same Holy Church and steadfast in the Catholic Faith, we may forever observe the poverty and humility of our Lord Jesus Christ and of his most holy Mother, together with the holy Gospel, as we have firmly promised. Amen.

286. Similar is the situation with the rule of the Third Order. Of the earliest versions which have come down to us no one can say which is the more closely the rule St. Francis laid down for the Third Order in 1221. The Capestrano, the Koenigsberg, and the Mariano rules have come to us with evident àdditions. So has the Venetian rule, discussed and edited by Fr. Benvenuto Bughetti O.F.M. in AR XIV (1921) pp. 109-121. But the latter rule, by comparison, appears more basic and unadulterated than any other so far found. We use it as our original. The eight heads we use are, in sense, those of the Venetian codex.

Most people will know that St. Francis did not found a Third Order Regular, following the convent life. The Order of Continents ("those who refrained from certain things") or Penitents ("those turning to God from sinful or idle worldly pursuits") was founded explicitly for people living in the world. But its aptitude, its innate tendency, toward convent life led early to convent groupings of seculars.

The history of the Third Order rule is briefly as follows:

Pope Nicholas IV in 1289 clarified the confusion resulting from divergent local versions of the rule, by issuing a universally uniform rule (*Supra Montem*). This rule served the Third Order regular as well as secular until the days of Pope Leo X, who issued a special basic rule for the Third Order Regular in its various congregations (*Inter Cetera*, Jan. 20, 1521). This basic rule held for all groups of the regular or convent Third Order until Pope Pius XI in our day superseded it with a new basic rule in *Rerum Conditio* October 4, 1927.

The rule of the Third Order issued by Pope Nicholas IV in 1289 remained in force for the Third Order Secular until May 30, 1883, when Pope Leo XIII superseded it with the present rule (*Misericors Dei Filius*).

In all these versions and changes of the original rule there has been the sole purpose of adapting the spirit and as far as possible the letter of the original to the needs of the times, respectively of the group using the rule.

FIRST RULE OF THE THIRD ORDER

*Here beginneth the Rule of the Continent
Brothers and Sisters*

In the name of the Father and of the Son
and of the Holy Ghost. Amen.

The memorial of what is proposed by the
Brothers and Sisters of Penance living in
their own homes, begun in the year of our
Lord 1221, is as follows:

Chapter 1: Daily Life

1. The men belonging to this brotherhood
shall dress in humble, undyed cloth, the price
of which is not to exceed six Ravenna soldi an
ell, unless for evident and necessary cause a
temporary dispensation be given. And breadth
and thinness of the cloth are to be considered
in said price.

2. They shall wear their outer garments
and furred coats without open throat, sewed
shut or uncut but certainly laced up, not
open as secular people wear them; and shall
wear their sleeves closed.

3. The sisters in turn shall wear an outer
garment and tunic made of cloth of the same
price and humble quality; or at least they are
to have with the outer garment a white or
black underwrap or petticoat, or an ample
linen gown without gathers, the price of an
ell of which is not to exceed twelve Pisa

denars. As to this price, however, and the fur cloaks they wear a dispensation may be given according to the estate of the woman and the custom of the place. They are not to wear silken or dyed veils and ribbons.

4. And both the brothers and the sisters shall have their fur garments of lamb's wool only. They are permitted to have leather purses and belts sewed in simple fashion without silken thread, and no other kind. Also other vain adornments they shall lay aside at the bidding of the Visitor.

5. They are not to go to unseemly parties or to shows or dances. They shall not donate to actors, and shall forbid their household to donate.

Chapter 2: Abstinence

6. All are to abstain from meat save on Sundays, Tuesdays and Thursdays, except on account of illness or weakness, for three days at blood-letting, in traveling, or on account of a specially high feast intervening, namely, the Nativity for three days, New Year's, Epiphany, the Pasch of the Resurrection for three days, the Holy Apostles Peter and Paul, St. John the Baptist, the Assumption of the glorious Virgin Mary, the solemnity of All Hallows and of St. Martin. On the other days, when there is no fasting, they may eat cheese and eggs. But when they are with

religious in their convent homes, they have leave to eat what is served to them. And except for the feeble, the ailing and those traveling, let them be content with dinner and supper. Let the healthy be temperate in eating and drinking.

7. Before their dinner and supper let them say the Lord's prayer once, likewise after their meal, and let them give thanks to God. Otherwise let them say three Our Fathers.

Chapter 3: Fasting

8. From the Pasch of the Resurrection to the feast of All Hallows they are to fast on Friday. From the feast of All Hallows till Easter they are to fast on Wednesdays and Fridays, but still observing the other fasts enjoined in general by the Church.

9. They are to fast daily, except on account of infirmity or any other need, throughout the fast of St. Martin from after said day till Christmas, and throughout the greater fast from Carnival Sunday till Easter.

10. Sisters who are pregnant are free to refrain till their purification from the cor- poral observances except those regarding their dress and their prayers.

11. Those engaged in fatiguing work shall be allowed to take food three times a day from the Pasch of the Resurrection till the

Dedication feast of St. Michael. And when they work for others it will be allowed them to eat of everything served to them, except on Fridays and on the fasts enjoined in general by the Church.

Chapter 4: Prayer

12. All are daily to say the seven canonical Hours, that is Matins, Prime, Tierce, Sext, None, Vespers, and Compline. The clerics are to say them after the manner of the clergy. Those who know the Psalter are to say the Deus in nomine tuo and the Beati immaculati up to the Legem pone for the Prime, and the other psalms of the Hours, with the Glory be to the Father, but when they do not attend church, they are to say for the Matins the psalms the Church says or any other eighteen psalms; or at least to say the Our Father as do the unlettered at any of the Hours.

The others say twelve Our Fathers for the Matins and for every one of the other Hours seven Our Fathers with the Gloria Patri after each one. And those who know the Creed and the Miserere mei Deus should say it at the Prime and the Compline. If they do not say that at the Hours indicated, they shall say three Our Fathers.

13. The sick are not to say the Hours unless they wish.

14. All are to go to Matins in the fast of St. Martin and in the great fast, unless inconvenience for persons or affairs should threaten.

Chapter 5: The Sacraments, Other Matters

15. They are to make a confession of their sins three times a year and to receive Communion at Christmas, Easter, and Pentecost. They are to be reconciled with their neighbors and to restore what belongs to others. They are to make up for past tithes and pay future tithes.

16. They are not to take up lethal weapons, or bear them about, against anybody.

17. All are to refrain from formal oaths unless where necessity compels, in the cases excepted by the Sovereign Pontiff in his indult, that is, for peace, for the Faith, under calumny, and in bearing witness.

18. Also in their ordinary conversation they will do their best to avoid oaths. And should anyone have sworn thoughtlessly through a slip of the tongue as happens where there is much talking, he should the evening of the same day, when he is obliged to think over what he has done, say three Our Fathers in amends of such oaths. Let each member fortify his household to serve God.

Chapter 6: *Special Mass and Meeting Each Month*

19. All the brothers and sisters of every city and place are to foregather every month at the time the ministers see fit, in a church which the ministers will make known, and there assist at Divine services.

20. And every member is to give the treasurer one ordinary denar. The treasurer is to collect this money and distribute it on the advice of the ministers among the poor brothers and sisters, especially the sick and those who may have nothing for their funeral services, and thereupon among other poor; and they are to offer something of the money to the aforesaid church.

21. And, if it be convenient at the time, they are to have some religious who is informed in the word of God, to exhort them and strengthen them to persevere in their penance and in performing the works of mercy. And except for the officers, they are to remain quiet during the Mass and sermon, intent on the Office, on prayer and on the sermon.

Chapter 7: *Visiting the Sick, Burying the Dead*

22. Whenever any brother or sister happens to fall ill, the ministers—if the patient has let them know of it—shall in person or

through others visit the patient once a week, and remind him of penance; and if they find it expedient, they are to supply him from the common fund with what he may need for the body.

23. And if the ailing person depart from this life, it is to be published to the brothers and sisters who may be present in the city or place, so that they may gather for the funeral; and they are not to leave until the Mass has been celebrated and the body consigned to burial. Thereupon each member within eight days of the demise shall say for the soul of the deceased: a Mass if he is a priest, fifty psalms if he understands the Psalter, or if otherwise, fifty Our Fathers with the Requiem aeternam at the end of each.

24. In addition, every year, for the welfare of the brothers and sisters living and dead, each priest is to say three Masses, each member knowing the Psalter is to recite it, and the rest shall say 100 Our Fathers with the Requiem aeternam at the end of each. Otherwise let them duplicate . . .

25. All who have the right, are to make their last will and make disposition of their goods within three months after their profession, lest anyone of them die intestate.

26. As regards making peace among the brothers and sisters or non-members at odds,

let what the ministers find proper be done; even, if it be expedient, upon consultation with the Lord Bishop.

27. If contrary to their right and privileges trouble is made for the brothers and sisters by the mayors and governors of the places where they live, the ministers of the place shall do what they shall find expedient on the advice of the Lord Bishop.

28. Let each member accept and faithfully exercise the ministry or other offices imposed on him, although anyone may retire from office after a year.

29. When anybody wishes to enter this brotherhood, the ministers shall carefully inquire into his standing and occupation, and they shall explain to him the obligations of the brotherhood, especially that of restoring what belongs to others. And if he is content with it, let him be vested according to the prescribed way, and he must make satisfaction for his debts, paying the money according to what pledged provision is given. They are to reconcile themselves with their neighbors and to pay up their tithes.

30. After these particulars are complied with, when the year is up and he seems suitable to them, let him on the advice of some discreet brothers be received on this condition: that he promise he will all the time of his

life observe everything here written, or to be written or abated on the advice of the brothers, unless on occasion there be a valid dispensation by the ministers; and that he will, when called upon by the ministers, render satisfaction as the Visitor shall ordain if he have done anything contrary to this condition. And this promise is to be put in writing then and there by public notary. Even so nobody is to be received otherwise, unless in consideration of the estate and rank of the person it shall seem advisable to the ministers.

31. No one is to depart from this brotherhood and from what is contained herein, except it be to enter a religious order.

32. No heretic or person in bad repute for heresy is to be received. If he is under suspicion of it, he may be admitted if otherwise fit upon being cleared before the Bishop.

33. Married women are not to be received except with the consent and leave of their husbands.

34. Brothers and sisters ejected from the brotherhood as incorrigible, are not to be received in it again except it please the saner portion of the brothers.

Chapter 8: Correction, Dispensation, Officers

35. The ministers of any city or place shall report public faults of the brothers and sisters

to the Visitor for punishment. And if anyone proves incorrigible, after consultation with some of the discreet brothers he should be denounced to the Visitor, to be expelled by him from the brotherhood, and thereupon it should be published in the meeting. Moreover, if it is a brother, he should be denounced to the mayor or the governor.

36. If anyone learns that scandal is occurring relative to brothers and sisters, he shall report it to the ministers and shall have opportunity to report it to the Visitor. He need not be held to report it in the case of husband against wife.

37. The Visitor has the power to dispense all the brothers and sisters in any of these points if he finds it advisable.

38. When the year has passed, the ministers with the counsel of the brothers are to elect two other ministers; and a faithful treasurer, who is to provide for the need of the brothers and sisters and other poor; and messengers who at the command of the ministers are to publish what is said and done by the fraternity.

39. In all the above mentioned points no one is to be obligated under guilt, but under penalty; yet so that if after being admonished twice by the ministers he should fail to discharge the penalty imposed or to be imposed

on him by the Visitor, he shall be obligated under guilt as contumacious.

Here endeth the Rule of the Continent

At this point other versions of the rule add their local "items," that is, their special regulations for the local fraternity.

Beatus fraciscus duobz ānie ante mōte sua fecit quadra
gesimā i loco d lueme ad honorē beate vīginis māie mahī dizbeab
michael archagli a festo assūptiois see māie igis usg ad festū sci
micgael septisb; 7 facta est sup eū man dni pr uisione 7 allocuti
onē feraphy 7 impssione stigmatūx icope suo fet has laudes ex alio
latere beatule scplas 7 manu sua scpsit gias agēs dode bnsiciosibi
collato Benedicat tibi dns i cusso

diatte_ ostē dat faciem

suā tibi 1 misereaf tui.

cōuertat iuiltu suū ad te

i det nbi pacē ~aw

ℭ Beat fraciscs scnptus manu sua istā bndictione mfri leōi

dns bene
flete te dicat

ℭ Simili modo fecit istud signū thau eū capite manu sua

The Blessing of Brother Leo

See Nos. 34 and 35, and Note 34

*NOTES

16. Ubertino da Casale, *Tree of the Crucified Life of Jesus*, summing up passages from *Sacrum Commercium S. Francisci cum Domina Paupertate* (Q. 1929), especially paragraphs 19-21; also LF 13; B 7. See **49.**

18. "Place" here and elsewhere is Francis's name for convent or friary.

19. Let the sophisticated not smirk when they read of such welcome to suffering as St. Francis shows here and elsewhere throughout this book. To the healthy instincts of saints and other people like Francis, pain and suffering remain just that as long as they live. Their senses shrink from it. It is not their senses, but only calculated will and choice which welcome it, by way of counteraction and expiation for overindulgent senses and by way of making their person resemble their crucified Savior. Theirs is the welcome of grace, not of that utter perversion of senses which seeks physical pleasure in suffering.

23. The ejaculation, "My God and my all," bears an indulgence of 300 days.—Preces et Pia Opera (1950) no. 5.

34. One day, says Thomas of Celano (2, 49),

when St. Francis was in retirement in his cell on Mt. La Verna, "one of his companions" wished greatly to have a souvenir of some words of our Lord briefly noted down in the handwriting of St. Francis. Francis said to him: "Bring me paper and ink, for I want to write down the words of God and his praises, on which I have been meditating in my heart."

He wrote down the words he wished, and added a blessing for the brother, saying, "Take this little sheet of paper and keep it carefully to the day of your death."

The sheet itself as preserved, tells, in Brother Leo's hand and words, that he was the brother and companion who received the souvenir, and that it was written after the Stigmata had been bestowed. Miracles were wrought with the page containing the words: a grievous temptation suffered by Brother Leo himself was dissipated by it.

One side of the page bears the Praises, the other side bears the blessing to Brother Leo. Of the latter only the last part is in the hand of Francis; the first part was dictated to Brother Leo. See the reproduction preceding these Notes.

Distinguish this "Page of Praises of God to Brother Leo" from "The Praises or Lauds of God in the Our Father," as in **36.**

52. To Francis everything worthless was "fly" or "brother fly," particularly also money.

55. The letter to St. Anthony is now accepted as genuine in contents and form as well as in fact (see *Franziskanische Studien*, 1949, p. 135

on). It was written early in 1224, before St. Anthony developed his great apostolate in southern France. Note that to St. Francis the properly disposed teacher of theology is a "bishop"!

68. That is, "die to himself," by mortification, self abnegation.

70. See entry Written Words of God in the Topical Index.

80. See Note 210 below.

86. Apart from separate mention of God and of the persons Father, Son, and Holy Ghost singly, the whole Blessed Trinity will be found invoked in one form or another in marginal numbers 28, 34, 36 twice, 36a twice, 37 to 37q repeatedly (after each psalm; note also 37a), 81, 117, 141, 192, 192f, 192h, 192k, 230, 230j, 230p, 231, 232, 282i, 283a, 283w, 283-4, 283-7, 283-9 twice, 283-10 twice.

He loved to have mention of Mary in his work, speech and writings, as in nos. 11, 16, 37, 37a, 37q; 65, 66, 67, 76, 82, 89, 97, 122, 159, 163, 191, 192d, 192h, 230a, 231 to 234, 261; 270 and 277, 283o, 283-9 twice, 285a, 285e, 285g.

Similarly he liked the inspiration and company of the angels and saints: the angel choirs 37a, 267, 283-9; St. Michael 37a, 86, 283-1, 283-9, the Michaelmas fast; St. Gabriel 230a, 283-9; St. Raphael 283-9; All Saints 98b, 283g, 283-9, the All Saints fast; all the ranks of saints 283-9; St. Peter 87, Sts. Peter and Paul 49, 87, 283-9; St. John Baptist 192d, 283-9; St. John Evangelist 283-9; St. Lawrence 63; St. Martin, in the fast 285d, 286c2, 286c3.

104. See entry Poverty in the Topical Index.

146. See note 210.

150. There is an indulgence of 7 years if this act of adoration is made in this form on bended knees when entering or when leaving a church or a public (or semi-public—for those whom it serves) oratory. There is a plenary indulgence if at least once a day the act is performed for an entire month; confession, communion, and prayer for the intention of the Pope being also required. —PPO (1950) 95.

There is a shorter form in honor of the Passion: "We adore you, O Christ, and bless you; because by your holy cross you have redeemed the world." An indulgence of 3 years is granted for the prayer in this form; an indulgence of 10 years if the Apostles' Creed is said with it, out of devotion to the suffering and death of our Lord. A plenary indulgence is granted under the usual conditions if the prayer is said daily for a month.—PPO (1950) 191

192. The minister general was Brother Elias.

192f. Other manuscripts have here, or intimate here with initials, the addition of the word "Roman" before the word "Church."

The words, as the Q editors and also the Bollandists point out, are by no means directed against so called private Masses, but refer to the Roman rite, in which Francis preferred that no more than one Mass be celebrated on any day.

In the very next words Francis tells what he would like to see when several priests are present; each for charity's sake should hear the Mass of

the other (alter ... alterius, each ... the other's
Mass), since Christ has favors for the worthy at
every Mass, and several Masses do not put him
under limitations as to what he will give those
who attend.

208. We have never found a satisfactory ex-
planation of the source and authorship of this
prayer. The nearest approach to it in early
Franciscan writings is found in the *Sayings of
Brother Giles*, who joined St. Francis in 1209 and
died a blessed death in 1262. He was a stalwart
friend and imitator of St. Francis, and very like
him in native and inspired wisdom. The very first
chapter of his Sayings as published by the Q
editors contains a passage which strongly recalls
the Peace Prayer. Is it an echo of the teachings of
St. Francis?

Here are the words:
"If you love, you will be loved; if you respect
people, you will be respected; if you serve them,
you will be served; if you give a good account of
yourself toward others, others will act likewise
toward you. Blessed the man who loves and
does not desire to be loved for it; blessed he who
respects them and does not look for respect in
return; who serves and does not expect service
for it; who acquits himself well of others and does
not desire that they return the grace. Because
such things are big, foolish people do not rise to
them."—Dicta B. Aegidii Assisiensis, 2nd edition,
1939, Q.

210. Fundamental to the public apostolate of
St. Francis and his disciples were two considera-

tions—considerations which were fundamental also to life in the order itself. The considerations were: 1.) utter submissiveness to the Church, in the person of Pope, Bishop, Priest and Clergy generally, as the minister and interpreter of the Gospel and the Faith; 2) deep, consistent, practical personal faith, and that most of all in Christ as really present in the Blessed Sacrament. Precisely the most authentic documents we have on St. Francis, his writings, bear out both points. His rules, his Testament, his letters are permeated with both thoughts. As to the former see the Topical Index under such entries as Church, Clergy, Pope, Cardinal Protector, Priest.

As to the Blessed Sacrament, devotion to it was at the base of his respect for churches as the dwelling places of our Lord, for the priesthood, for the words of God, for the sacred utensils, while it was the main topic of his Letter to the Chapter General, of that to the Custodes, and of that to All the Clergy, at the same time that it is prominent as a topic in the Testament, in all the Rules, in the Reminders, and in the letters to All the Faithful and to Public Officials. See these several items as listed in the Table of Contents, and also the passages listed under the entry Blessed Sacrament in the Topical Index.

Indeed there have been those who have regarded the entire Franciscan Movement, in the order and before the public, as dominated by the Eucharistic idea, employed as the means to tame and Christianize a people enthusiastic for the outer forms of the Faith indeed, but lacking the deeper convictions and sense of it. It is not without relevance that devotion to the Blessed Sacrament has remained characteristic of the children of St. Francis to this day, and that Perpetual Adoration so regularly forms a part of the life not only of the contemplative Poor Clares but also of the very active life of the convent Third Order. If in the rules of St. Francis governing reception of the Holy Eucharist a, to us, low minimum of incidence is indicated, it was an advanced demand for a minimum at the time, with back of it the outstanding, burning, seraphic zeal of St. Francis as found in his writings urging ever greater fervor toward the Savior in our midst, the Babe of Greccio, the crucified Seraph of La Verna imprinting His likeness on those who draw near to Him.

216. Here as elsewhere (191, 192g, 205) St. Francis is thinking of God's almighty power equal alike to creating the human body, to endowing it with grace in the Incarnation and Redemption, and to making present the Body and Blood of our Lord under the forms of bread and wine in the Holy Eucharist. All three mysteries interlock in Divine intention and effect, all "sanctify the body," whether we take "body" as referring to the ordinary human person (in the language of the day of Francis *corpus*, or body, and person are often the same concept, as when we say no-body, every-body, or habeas corpus) sanctified by God's grace dwelling in it; or as referring to the human body and soul of Christ sanctified by union with the Person of God the Son; or as referring to the sacramental forms sanctified inasmuch as the Incarnate Word replaces their substance with his. Always of course in these passages the stress is on the mystery of the Holy Eucharist, and the thought is of the almighty Fiat required to "sanctify the body" in the respective sense while the conclusion is: As we venerate these sacred mysteries, so let us give glory to the Word of God which calls them forth, and in token of that glory let us respect the material forms or symbols, "the written word," in which they are conveyed to us, most of all if the writings are sacred.

220. The AN editors in a footnote at this point (page 215) show at what period in the life of Ugolino, St. Dominic and St. Francis this meeting could have occurred between the time when Cardinal Ugolino was appointed privately as Cardinal Protector following the summer of 1217 and the death of St. Dominic August 6, 1221. In the four years there was repeated opportunity for such a meeting in Rome, though just when the meeting took place cannot be determined. St. Dominic was in Rome at five points in that time. To date no valid reason has been found to discredit the tradition of the meeting.

233. Found in the Wadding-de la Haye Opera Omnia S.P.N.F. p. 18; maintained as authentic by Sabatier in *Opuscules de Critique Hist.*, fasc. X, p. 164.

253. If Fr. Bartholomew of Pisa were writing in our time, he could add a further conformity to the many he found between our Lord and his counterpart St. Francis. He could find it precisely in the way our Lord and St. Francis have been treated by "higher critics" of the past century.

In the effort to be rid of our Lord's doctrine they have disputed his Divinity and to supply a basis for disputing his Divinity they have advanced the most fantastic, well, let us say ingenious, theories as to the authority of the Scriptures, their authorship, time and place of their origin and the process of their being pieced together. Regularly, however, closer investigation has the traditional view on these particulars stand out with fresh luster.

Similarly with St. Francis. In this past century there has been the strange obsession in certain quarters that St. Francis had found an ideal for living the Gospel life which could have done wonders for the regeneration of the world, had not a reactionary Church and her henchman dignitaries prevented Francis from realizing the ideal. What the ideal consisted in beyond what we have in the writings, sayings and actions of Francis as traditionally recognized, they do not tell us exactly. Neither do they say just how the Church thwarted the work of St. Francis; but she must have done so because spirits of a later generation to which they are sympathetic fell out with Mother Church on that plea!

In any case the Church took the order away from St. Francis and gave it to a set more compliant with the Church, reducing Francis to the position of a frustrated genius for the last years of his life. If this view flies in the face of all recorded fact and six hundred years of tradition, well, you just go to work on the records and show by whatever ingenuity you can bring to bear how the records have been pieced together! Well-meaning men are caught up in the drift, and feel they must follow suit.

Theory has followed theory, especially since Sabatier's day (roughly, 1890). But each new "find" on closer inspection leaves the traditional sources just as they were. One after another the radical views have gone by the boards, including those of John R. H. Moorman as advanced in *The Sources of the Life of St. Francis of Assisi*. With the latter Fr. Michael Bihl dealt decisively in AR XXXIX (1946, sole issue) pp. 3 to 27 and pp. 279-287. The same distinguished critic, in AR XLI p. 296 dealt similarly with the theory advanced in Karrer's *Franz von Assisi—Legenden und Laude:* Karrer's theory on the text he uses to cover the early years of St. Francis is the exploded Lazzeri theory of 1923.

At the present stage of the controversy there is as little reason for departure from the traditional acceptance of St. Francis sources as there is for discarding the Gospels as authentic records. And Francis remains what these true sources make him out to be—a great saint of the Catholic Church, which, with all that stands for it and all it stands for, he revered and loved and heeded as Christ incorporated.

This virtue we must vindicate for Francis against the prevailing affectation, especially in English-speaking countries, of seeing Francis as a rebel. Unfortunately, it is the popular attitude to see the Church at the opposite pole of Christ, and for years to come it will remain the popular attitude to regard, of all people, St. Francis as antagonized by the Church and resenting it.

261. Concepts naturally without sex, receive gender by grammatical and poetic convention. Romance tongues may have a *la* for their *Morte* in grammar, but as to poetry and art generally it is doubtful whether anything would serve them but the Horseman, the Reaper, the Man with the Scythe, Father Time. Usage has left Death neuter in English, but poetically he is definitely masculine and also grammatically his lineal sire is Germanic *Der Tod* with collateral kin like Greek *Ho Thanatos*. So, "Brother" Death in English he shall be.

281. To get at the true signification of The Canticle of Brother Sun, recall from **271** the lament of St. Francis that men use God's creatures to offend him with them when they should be taking occasion to honor him with them. This note his theme expresses in the first stanza of The Canticle: God, and God alone, deserves praise, and deserves it from every source. So Francis would have all creatures, led by most distinguished Brother Sun, giving honor to God through man's good use instead of his abuse of their several qualities and functions.

In this sense understand the *cum* in line one of the Brother Sun stanza, and the *per* which keeps recurring with each new creature mustered: The praise and honor are not to go *to* the creatures (Robinson's unhappy: "especially *to* my brother sun"); it is not to be *shared by* the creatures—the *cum* or *with* in the Brother Sun stanza is used in the sense of instrumentality, not of accompaniment ("be praised," not along with, but "by means of" them); it is not, either, "be praised *for*" the creatures mentioned farther on—the *per* there is the old (as well as modern) Italian, meaning "through," "by means of," just as in line 3 of the Sun stanza, line 3 of the Wind stanza, and line 2 of the Fire stanza.

As long ago as 1875 Matthew Arnold (*Essays in Criticism*) pointed out this true meaning of the words. In his translation he got around the cumbersome "by means of," the less exact and too exclusive "by," and the rough "through" by using the poetic "of"—"Be praised of Sister Moon, of Brother Wind, etc. Karrer (Legends and Lauds) in the original German uses *durch*, "through"; so do Esser-Hardick in their (1951) *Schriften des hl. Franziskus von Assisi*, Dietrich Coelde-Verlag, Werl. In 1941 Benedetto's *Il Cantico di Frate Sole*, Firenze, called attention to these points, also to the *cum* in the Sun stanza, as denoting "by means of." In English, "with" could stand if all would understand it as "by means of," as should be.

We have taken the liberty to use "of" and "through" at the critical points, to exclude misunderstanding as far as possible.

We use as our original an old Italian text discussed and reproduced in AR, XLI, pp. 1-87. Originals and copies of The Canticle of Brother Sun are consistent in neither meter, nor rhyme, nor line grouping.

282. See note 150.

TOPICAL INDEX

The numbers refer to the marginal series